THE BOOK OF
BUTTONS

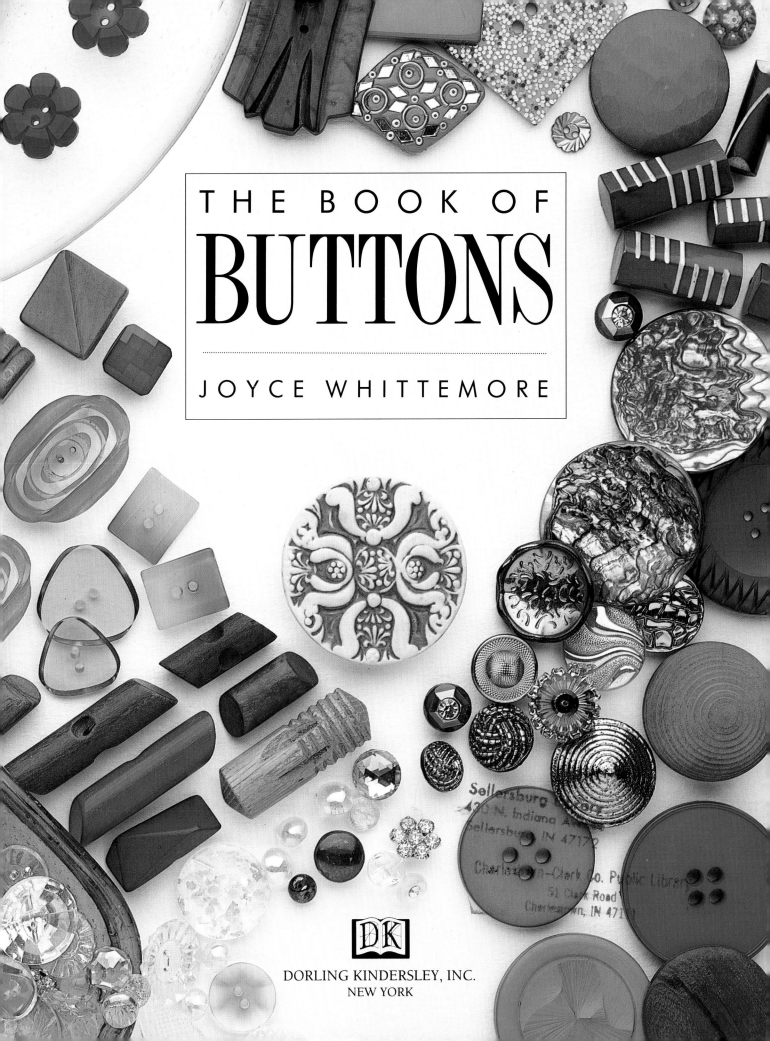

THE BOOK OF
BUTTONS

JOYCE WHITTEMORE

DORLING KINDERSLEY, INC.
NEW YORK

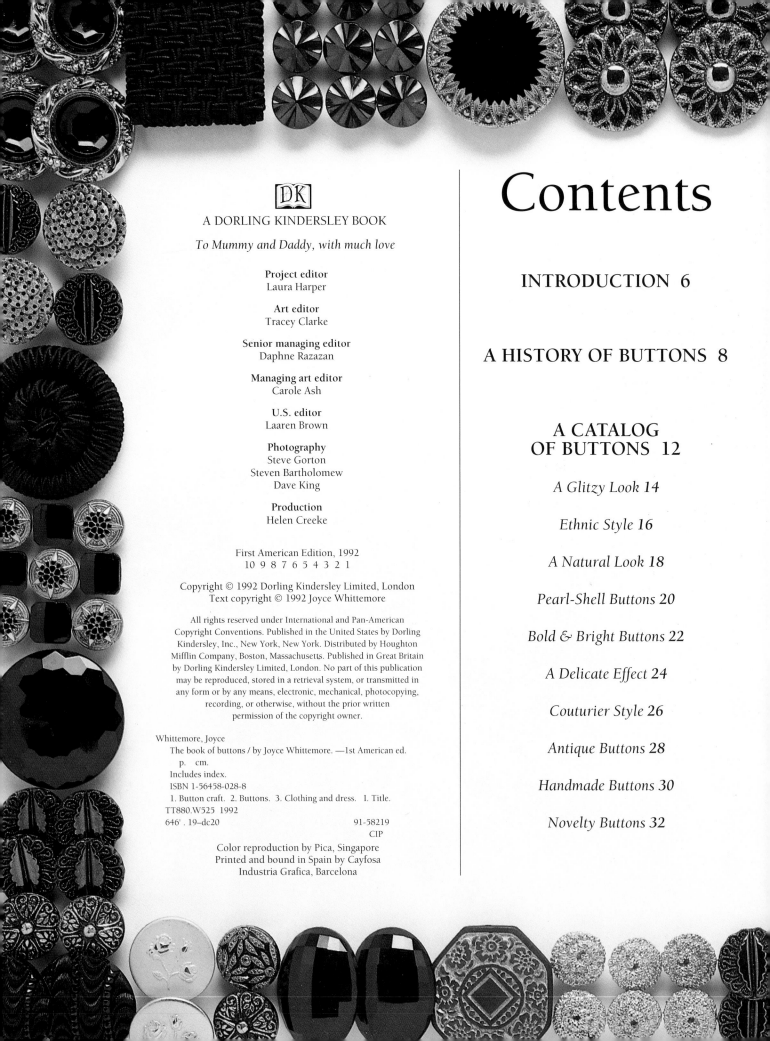

DK

A DORLING KINDERSLEY BOOK

To Mummy and Daddy, with much love

Project editor
Laura Harper

Art editor
Tracey Clarke

Senior managing editor
Daphne Razazan

Managing art editor
Carole Ash

U.S. editor
Laaren Brown

Photography
Steve Gorton
Steven Bartholomew
Dave King

Production
Helen Creeke

First American Edition, 1992
10 9 8 7 6 5 4 3 2 1

Whittemore, Joyce
    The book of buttons / by Joyce Whittemore. —1st American ed.
    p.   cm.
    Includes index.
    ISBN 1-56458-028-8
    1. Button craft. 2. Buttons. 3. Clothing and dress.   I. Title.
TT880.W525 1992
646'. 19–dc20   91-58219
                                                          CIP
Color reproduction by Pica, Singapore
Printed and bound in Spain by Cayfosa
Industria Grafica, Barcelona

Contents

Introduction

Nearly everyone wears buttons at one time or another, but how often do they appreciate the workmanship that goes into making even the simplest button? Ever since fastenings became necessary, buttons have been not only functional but also ornamental. Some are works of art in miniature, a tribute to the skill and craftsmanship of men and women through the ages.

Buttons have been made from any number of materials — wood, mother-of-pearl, glass, shell, leather, horn and bone, enamel, a variety of plastics, and even precious stones. Styles are equally wide-ranging, from plain classic buttons to the most outrageous fun buttons. Historically, the size and brilliance of the finished article has depended not simply on fashion but also on politics and religion. There are certain religious sects that will not wear buttons even today, considering them to be proud adornments worn out of vanity, while gypsies, on the other hand, believe buttons are lucky. Among primitive and sophisticated peoples the world over, buttons have been used decoratively, trimming hats in India, made into neckbands in Africa, sewn all over clothes by the pearly kings and queens in England, and used internationally for impressive effect on military uniforms, while in modern fashion there has been a recent vogue for clothes that are decorated and encrusted with buttons.

At one time most families had a button box, and many people can remember getting to play with the box as children. These boxes contained endless treasures, full of memories in the same way that a patchwork quilt can recall a particular dress or coat. In more recent years, changes resulting in women having less available time have led to a demand for easy-care items of clothing, and consequently to the advent of molded nylon and polyester buttons. At the same time, many craftsmen from the old school, who were making more interesting specialist buttons, retired, leaving no successors to continue their trade. People tended to throw away the buttons with their old clothes rather than cutting them off and saving them in the family button box.

It was at this point that I became involved in the button trade. I was employed as a textile designer, working on a line of gowns that required large dramatic fasteners. Looking for buttons was a revelation: There was nothing suitable in the stores, and the only good buttons to be found tended to be hidden away in forgotten corners of dusty old trimmings warehouses — valueless in the light of the modern obsession with functionality. The sheer variety of these old buttons in contrast to the paucity of what was available in stores for the general public was astounding, and later, wondering what I might sell in a market stand that I was planning to set up, I hit upon the idea of using the vast array of magnificent old buttons that I had discovered.

With happy memories of absorbing childhood hours spent playing with my own mother's box of buttons, I called the business Button Box. Borrowing a ridiculously small sum of money, I bought a whole warehouse attic's worth of Art Deco buttons and thousands of glass buttons from a gigantic storehouse in the East End of London. I eventually acquired a permanent place at Camden Lock, a popular craft market in London that, in those days, attracted not only the general public but also fashion designers. As I started to deal with the designers, I gradually gained an idea of the intense desire for new styles each season that motivated the fashion industry. Consequently, I began to search out specific stocks of buttons in response to designers' individual requests. Adhering to this principle of customized service, I built up the wholesale side of the business while still selling to the public through the outdoor market stand.

As stocks of old buttons started to dwindle, I looked around for new supplies. Help came in the person of a wonderful button manufacturer, whose love and knowledge of the button trade enabled him to work with me, producing small runs of specially made buttons. Together we created some unique styles for the designers, placing Button Box at the top of the button trade. I began to sell the remainders of the commissioned wholesale stocks of buttons at the Covent Garden market in London, and noticing a great demand for this type of button, I also opened a shop. By this time I was sourcing and buying craftsman-made buttons worldwide, and the small store quickly overflowed with thousands of varieties of beautiful and extraordinary buttons, and attracted many customers from all over the world.

This book is a celebration of buttons, and although it can show only a tiny cross section, it is designed to illustrate the incredible range of buttons that has been and is available, and to encourage creative appreciation and decorative use of buttons. I hope that as a result of reading this book, more people will be encouraged to look at buttons not only as a functional necessity but also as tiny ornaments to be used in an adventurous and imaginative way. Buttons should be bold, brilliant, basic, or beautiful, but never, never boring.

A History of Buttons

Fourteenth century

1500s–1600s

1300s–1400s

Times past
Many old metal buttons, including the top two here, have been discovered on the shores of the River Thames. The first depicts a person praying (now just visible); the six-petaled flower was probably ornamental rather than functional; and the intriguing loop button may have been worn on a sleeve.

I t seems likely that as soon as man needed to hold together two pieces of fabric or fur, he used his ingenuity to invent buttons. Their exact origins are unclear, but archeologists have found what they believe to be prehistoric buttons. Ancient Greeks and Etruscans are thought to have used buttons and loops to fasten garments at the shoulder, and early Persians buttoned their boots. From the start, buttons have been valued not only as fasteners. Fashioned from many materials and incorporating the myriad skills of master craftsmen through the ages, they can be as splendid to look at, as innovative and as precious as jewelry.

THE INFLUENCE OF THE EAST

The modern button, manufactured in large quantities, began life in the thirteenth century, when the revolutionary invention of the buttonhole replaced the loop fastening. Returning to their native lands, Crusaders brought back these innovations from the Middle East, and loose, flowing garments became more close-fitting, tightly secured with buttons from chin to waist and elbow to knuckle for men; women began to wear long, elegant, tightly buttoned fitted sleeves. The nobility adorned their clothes with buttons made of gold, silver, and copper, decoratively inset with precious ivory, tortoiseshell, and jewels; the general populace wore more functional fabric or thread buttons.

In Paris, buttonmakers were formed into guilds, and in each the crafts-men worked in only those materials they had been trained to use: base metal; ivory, horn, and bone; or precious metals and glass. Similar guilds formed in other parts of Europe, and, by the fourteenth century, craftsman-made buttons were an established part of the economy. Much of this trade was in luxury buttons, until, in Italy, sumptuary laws (restraining extravagant living) forbade the excessive use of buttons for personal adornment, and specified that cloth or silver buttons only were to be worn.

FOR KINGS AND COMMONERS

During the fifteenth and sixteenth centuries, cheaper materials — bone, wood, brass, and pewter — brought decorative buttons within the reach of more people, and, by the late sixteenth century, copper, brass, iron, pewter, and tin decorated military uniforms. The rich continued to wear costly, custom-made sets of buttons, which became more sumptuous and stone-encrusted as the Renaissance influenced Europe.

From the sixteenth century on, buttonmakers were patronized by royalty, including Francis I of France, who wore a garment ornamented with 13,600 golden buttons, and Louis XIV, who paid an enormous sum for six buttons. During this period, valuable buttons were often not secured with thread: Shanks were pushed through holes on the garment's button band and fastened with a metal strip threaded through the back. This allowed the buttons to be moved from garment to garment.

Enameled buttons
Enameling techniques were first applied to buttons in sixteenth-century Limoges; early examples were worn by Francis I. Once cheaper methods of production were perfected, buttons like this nineteenth-century example became more widely available.

CROSSING THE ATLANTIC

In Colonial America, buttons were imported largely from Britain, owing to British trade restrictions. The devout faith and simple lives of some of the first European settlers, many of them Quakers and Puritans, dictated simple, functional buttons.

As life became more luxurious for some members of the new American community, and as fashion became more flamboyant during the 1700s, European-style buttons were imported. American-produced buttons were mostly made in metal by jewelers or silversmiths, but other artisans, such as clockmakers, made buttons as a sideline. A wave of patriotism inspired by the Revolutionary War led American manufacturers to increase production of metal buttons, and to experiment with other materials such as varnished papier-mâché, in an attempt to reduce imports.

BUTTONS AND THE LAW

Fabric and embroidered buttons became fashionable throughout Europe in the seventeenth century. Small in size, these buttons were used in large numbers mainly for decorative effect, sewn in many rows around wide sleeves, or down the front of a long, full-skirted man's coat. To protect the silk industry in Paris and Lyons, French law insisted that buttons be covered in silk, while in England, from the late 1600s until the early 1700s, laws prohibited fabric buttons, insisting on metal to encourage the industry.

TINY WORKS OF ART

As the eighteenth century progressed, buttons became more popular. Men wore large quantities of buttons in lines down their long narrow coats, and the adoption of a double-breasted style allowed even more buttons to be worn, all highly conspicuous and purely ornamental, since only two or three fastened. Scenes were painted on porcelain and ivory buttons, set in glass or metal frames, and sold in silk-lined cases. The subject matter often reflected contemporary life — fashions in hair and costume, architecture — and displayed the penchant for romantic landscapes, mythological scenes peopled with cupids, and the imaginary idyllic shepherds and shepherdesses so beloved by Marie Antoinette and her court.

Habitat buttons, made from grasses, flowers, shells, stones, and even insects mounted under glass, provide us with antique relics from nature, and rebus buttons show the mania for mottoes and riddles, inscribed, most often, on the theme of love.

Real-life buttons
A miniature "snapshot" of history, this French button depicts the storming of the Bastille.

Ornamental buttons
Worn in large numbers, fabric buttons were an essential part of the seventeenth-century European gentleman's wardrobe. The next century saw the zenith of magnificent fancy buttons.

The button industry
New processes invented and patented for making buttons in the 1700s and 1800s in England sometimes proved hazardous to the workers. At the same time, they placed British manufacturers at the forefront of the metal button trade and benefited the metal industry.

British button kings
London's traditional "pearly king" outfits were invented by street vendors in the late 1800s. Designers are still influenced by their button-encrusted style.

THE MECHANIZATION OF BUTTON-MAKING

Great advances were made in the mechanical manufacture of buttons in the eighteenth and nineteenth centuries. In Britain, competition gave rise to new machinery and new methods of stamping, molding, and casting metal buttons; many of these techniques remain in use today. In Dorset, Huguenot refugees skilled in lace-making turned their hands to producing buttons, and by the late 1700s a cottage industry flourished.

Dorset thread buttons sold worldwide well into the nineteenth century, but when machine-made linen buttons were patented after the Great Exhibition of 1851, hundreds of workers were out of business overnight.

The increase in early nineteenth-century U.S. domestic button production led manufacturers in Connecticut, the metal button center, to import English machinery. However, the skills it required were guarded jealously by the British, and only the migration of metal workers and industrial espionage enabled the Army to have domestically produced gilt uniform buttons for the War of 1812.

WOMEN BUTTON UP

Button-wearing was a male prerogative until the mid-1800s, when men's clothes became less flamboyant and gilt buttons, considered vulgar, were replaced by more restrained buttons of pearl, pewter, and jacquard fabric. When Parisian *haute couture* became influential in mid-century, buttons for women came into their own as fasteners and for decoration.

Following the widowhood of Queen Victoria and subsequent laws covering mourning dress, black clothing and jet and glass jet buttons became fashionable. China buttons were decorated to match calico prints for puritanical sections of American society that preferred invisible buttons. Horn button manufacture increased, too, with rough slices of horn used to make "bark" buttons for men's country sporting wear.

EXTRAVAGANCE AND FASHION

While men's fashion became more sober toward the end of the 1800s, women's wear became more extravagant. In the Gay Nineties, large, ornate celluloid or jeweled buttons adorned cloaks. By the early twentieth century, advances in world communications inspired fashion, and the influx and exhibition of objects from Japan was a formative influence on Art Nouveau, a revolt against technology and the heavy, solid designs of the last century. Beautiful buttons with soft, fluid lines depicted women's heads, drapery, and organic motifs. In turn, the Arts and Crafts movement idealized a revival of natural crafts and manufacturing methods to produce unique items, including handmade wooden buttons.

Parisian designers, increasingly influential, were greatly affected by artistic and cultural events. The Ballet Russe, for example, inspired a spate of Russian-style garments, buttoned asymmetrically, and the 1925 exhibition of decorative arts in Paris gave birth to Art Deco, which, with the introduction of American jazz, the functional ideas of the German Bauhaus movement, and the growing emancipation of women, changed fashion irrevocably from the fluid lines of the *belle époque* to the clean, square look of the 1920s and 1930s. Made, using new techniques, from the recently developed plastics Bakelite and casein, stunning buttons appeared in an explosion of color and bold geometric shapes.

Arts and Crafts buttons
Buttons hand-crafted by Fred Partridge from ebony, holly, rosewood, and walnut were made for individual customers. They matched the hand-woven fabrics typical of the movement.

FUNCTIONAL BUTTONS

As more women went to work, clothing became more functional. Styles such as the feminine version of a man's suit required simple buttons. During the Second World War, when raw materials were particularly scarce, buttons were simply utilitarian, and although the demand for buttons increased after the war, materials and skilled workers were in short supply. Ingenuity was needed to produce buttons. One manufacturer bought up plastic windshields from obsolete bombers; another made plaster buttons in gelatin molds on his bedroom floor. In the 1950s couturiers reopened their salons, and Chanel instituted her inimitable hallmark of distinctive gold buttons, reviving a vogue for metal buttons. Casein was widely used in the late 1940s and 1950s, but required handwork, and the increased demand for ready-made clothes encouraged manufacturers to look for alternative materials such as nylon and polyester.

When enthusiasm for versatile, easy-care items took precedence over design, casein fell into disuse, and quality was sacrificed for quantity. Production increased to such a dramatic extent that buttons had to be of uniform shape and size to allow them to be sewn on by machine. The demise of quality buttons was not halted until the late 1970s, when innovative young designers experimented with decorative buttons, using them not only for classic looks but also in more outrageous ways. During the punk era, for example, Vivienne Westwood used buttons in the same surrealistic way as Schiaparelli had in the 1930s. Because exclusive buttons were widely used by fashion designers in the 1980s, European manufacturers produced exquisite buttons again, and the era of the fancy button returned. However, in recent years manufacturers from the Far East have flooded the market with inferior copies of quality buttons. Because button manufacturers worldwide cannot compete with Far Eastern prices, their only option is to lead the field in design excellence, thus ensuring the survival of distinctive and decorative buttons.

Surreal buttons
In the 1930s, Elsa Schiaparelli, a designer involved in the Surrealist movement, created extraordinary buttons for her garments: rows of butterflies in ascending size; tiny glass boxes with lids, filled with coffee beans and rice. These plumed horse buttons adorned a 1938 jacket decorated with circus designs.

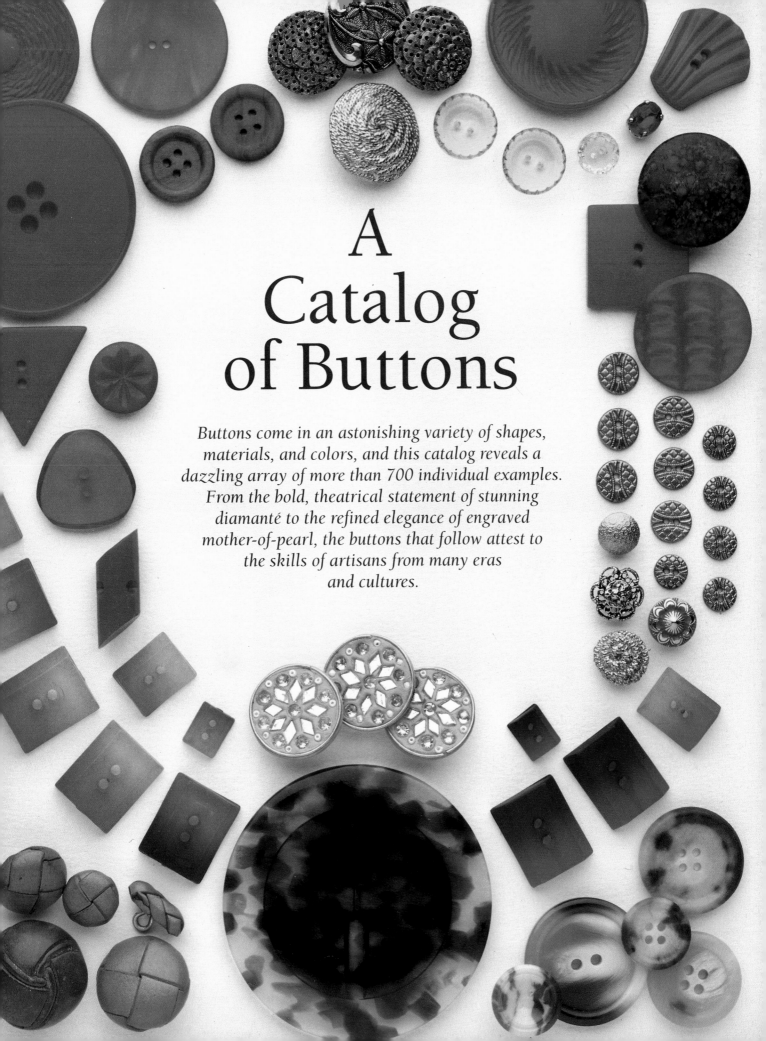

A Catalog of Buttons

Buttons come in an astonishing variety of shapes, materials, and colors, and this catalog reveals a dazzling array of more than 700 individual examples. From the bold, theatrical statement of stunning diamanté to the refined elegance of engraved mother-of-pearl, the buttons that follow attest to the skills of artisans from many eras and cultures.

A Glitzy Look

Glass, metal, and synthetics combine here to produce sparkle and drama in an array of stunning buttons for evening wear. Many are hand-finished and used by top couturiers for instant glamour. Prices are accordingly high, though inexpensive copies are also available.

Glass and crystal buttons
Clear glass is sometimes molded to imitate crystal, but even with the help of mirrored backing it can never match crystal's unique radiance. Swarovski crystal, precision cut by machine, is considered the most brilliant.

Swarovski crystal

1930s and 1940s buttons, *right*
The hard material of these molded glass buttons makes fine detailing possible; the gold finish has been carefully applied by hand.

Fine detailing decorated with gold

Modern antique-look buttons, *below*
Made from synthetic materials, these buttons are generally lighter and cheaper than the originals they imitate. They are available in a wide range of styles.

Black molded glass button

Molded glass

Colored glass and crystal buttons
Gold or silver-foil backing shines through colored glass and crystal for extra sparkle; iridescent backing gives rainbow colors.

Silvered base to add glitter

Plastic cabochon set in metallized nylon

Molded glass with iridescent backing

Plastic stone set in metallized nylon

Pearlized balls held in place by diamanté

Claw-set diamanté
This type of diamanté is better quality, more durable and more expensive than the glued kind.

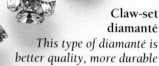

Large metal button with diamanté insets

Toggle

Jeweled colored glass
The color within this molded glass is mottled for a soft effect.

Decorated clear glass
Clear glass can be decorated with patterns etched or pressed into the reverse. The patterns are then painted or set off with mirrored backing.

Painted etching on the back

Gold reverse for mirror effect

Silver-foil backing seen from the front

1950s button with tie-tack backing

Glued diamanté
Clusters of glittering crystals or foil-backed stones are set into metal by hand with glue. The stones are not as secure as those set in claws.

Imitation pearl set in antique-look diamanté

Translucent color shows through the gilding

Solid-color center

Decorated glass buttons, *above*
These sumptuous-looking buttons are made of colored glass that has been pressed and then partially painted in gold or silver.

Imitation jet buttons
Queen Victoria began a craze for jet buttons after the death of Prince Albert. Imitation jet is made of molded glass, which is cold to the touch. Real jet feels warm.

Silver decoration on molded glass

Glass stones in metal create a peacock-tail effect

Jeweled buttons
These metal, glass, and nylon buttons are embellished with plain or multicolored stones.

Ethnic Style

From the mountains of Nepal and the mines of Brazil, from South Africa, Australia, and Sri Lanka come unique buttons, handcrafted and superbly finished in their country of origin. Made in small numbers from natural materials, with diverse and unusual designs, these are buttons of character and beauty. Indeed, some could be considered miniature works of art.

Elliptical toggle

Geometric shapes

Horn from Nepal
Craftsmen in the mountains of Nepal have fashioned especially dark horn into a selection of organic and geometric shapes to make these truly original buttons.

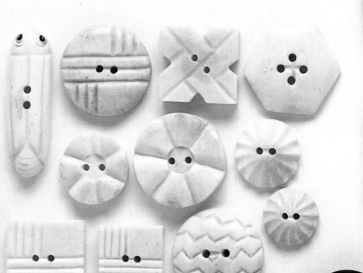

Nepalese bone
Cut from bone and hand-carved in simple yet effective patterns, these exquisite, delicate-looking buttons are, in reality, exceptionally durable.

Stained bone
Natural dyes tint these intricately carved bone buttons from Nepal.

Buttons from snakeskin
The skin is mounted on leather and disks cut. Each button has different markings.

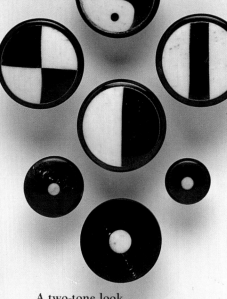

A two-tone look
These distinctive buttons in abstract designs are made of horn carefully inlaid with bone.

South African horn
The whitest pieces of this horn, waste from the meat industry, serve as chic imitation ivory. Darker pieces such as these lend a hand-worked feeling.

Mirrored glass

Bead

Gold braid

Copper wire

Decorative art from Rajasthan
For more than 200 years Indian jewelry and accessories have been handmade from lac, a resin secreted onto trees by insects. A small piece is heated over a charcoal fire until it becomes pliable. Powder dye is added and the substance put into a mold. Once cool, the blank is removed and decorated; beads and other tiny objects are heated and pressed into the surface with tweezers.

Curved shape symbolizes a person sitting, or shelter against the wind

Drawing from nature
Made by Australian aborigines, these clay buttons show aspects of "The Dreamtime," the traditional story of their ancient past. Here, dots represent rain, ants, or eggs; wavy lines mean a snake, smoke, flowing water, or lightning.

Amethyst

Granite

Hand-painting
This wooden button has been hand-painted with layers of oil-based paints. To prevent chipping, this kind of button should be removed before washing.

Hematite

Marble

Dolomite

Brazilian stone
A family business in Brazil's mountainous interior makes these buttons from semi-precious stone supplied by local mines. Craftsmen slice blanks and use diamond-tipped drills to make the holes.

Quartz

Sri Lankan demons
These humorous faces have been carved from wood and then hand-painted.

A Natural Look

The warm, muted tones and chunky shapes of buttons crafted from real wood, horn, leather, and even some types of nut complement winter handknits in neutral shades as well as casual tweed jackets. Less expensive alternatives, such as imitation horn and mock tortoiseshell, are also available.

Burned and milled wood

Stained, carved wood

Carved and milled wood
One method of enhancing wood is to stain and carve it; another is to char the surface over a flame and cut through the burned part to reveal the paler color beneath.

Light wood

Oak

Yew

Wood slices
The beauty of wood lies in its grain and textures, displayed in these buttons sliced from young branches and drilled with holes.

A selection of olive-wood buttons

Oiled wood

Stained wood

Ornamental olive-wood button

1960s hardwood button (natural color)

Wooden buttons
Blank disks are cut from sheets of wood, then turned and drilled. They are polished by tumbling in barrels and may be varnished. Unvarnished wood buttons should be removed from clothes before washing or dry-cleaning to prevent the natural oils from being stripped out. Olive wood, though, can survive several washes, since it contains more oil than other woods.

Treated wood
Light wood can be darkened with linseed oil, which soaks into the button, revealing the grain. Wood stains can also deepen the color of most types of wood.

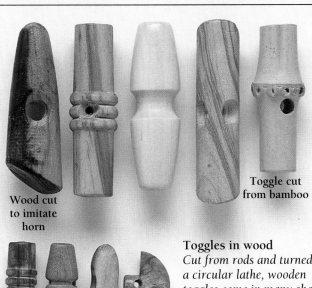

Wood cut to imitate horn

Toggle cut from bamboo

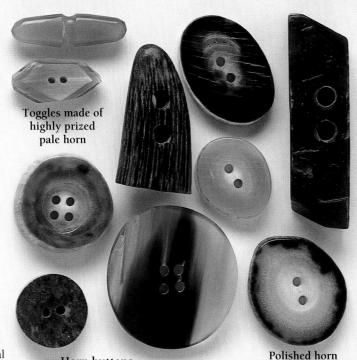

Toggles made of highly prized pale horn

Polished horn

Toggles in wood
Cut from rods and turned on a circular lathe, wooden toggles come in many shapes and sizes.

Horn buttons
A byproduct of the meat trade, horn for buttons comes from oxen or buffalo from the Far East, India, Africa, Argentina, and other Latin American countries. Variations in color depend on the country of origin; pale colors are the rarest. The outer bark may be stripped off or retained.

Petal fashioned from natural curve

Vegetable ivory (corozo nut)
The seed of this South American palm was used in button-making until the First World War, when it was discovered that rats were partial to buttons found in the trenches.

Coconut shell
The shell is smoothed and cut to make thin but tough buttons with immense character. The outer part of the shell is dark, the underside light.

Artificial horn
Made chiefly from polyester or casein, some copies can deceive, but many have such even patterns it is easy to spot a fake.

Mock tortoiseshell
Now that the hawksbill turtle is a protected species, tortoiseshell buttons are no longer produced. Instead, various synthetics are treated to resemble the shell.

Leather shank

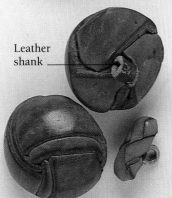

Leather buttons
"Football buttons" are traditionally made from strips of interwoven leather with a leather shank. Reconstituted leather makes smoother, but less durable, buttons.

Pearl-Shell Buttons

Among the most beautiful of all natural materials, pearl shell creates buttons rich in color and sheen. The buttons are drilled from ocean and freshwater shells from all over the world, once widely and inexpensively available as byproducts of the fishing industry, now threatened by increasingly polluted waters.

Dye makes irregular patterns on the shell back

Pearl-shell selection
Many types of shell are used in button-making, including mother-of-pearl (from the Australian pearl oyster) and abalone (also known as haliotis, or paua if from New Zealand).

Abalone

Dyed pearl-shell buttons
Mother-of-pearl and trochus buttons are colored with acid dyes and left to soak for a week to produce dark colors. After that time, the dye has penetrated only the surface.

Sliced button showing dye absorption

Mother-of-pearl

Back-to-front buttons
Some buttons are made with the shell side up, rather than the pearl side. Fashion designers use them for natural and ethnic looks.

Center turned on a lathe to reveal the pearl finish

Dyed burgos shell, partially polished

Abalone

An especially white 1920s freshwater pearl shell

Drilled pearl oyster shell
Blanks have been cut from this shell to produce mother-of-pearl buttons. Water is constantly splashed over the shell while it is being drilled, to prevent it from shattering. The best-quality buttons come from the thickest, and smallest, part of the shell.

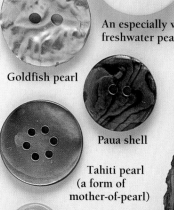

Goldfish pearl

Paua shell

Tahiti pearl (a form of mother-of-pearl)

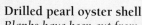

Freshwater pearl shell

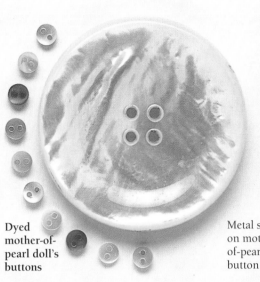

Trochus

Tooth-shaped trochus

Metal shank on mother-of-pearl shoe button

Shank glued to Tahiti pearl button

Dyed mother-of-pearl doll's buttons

Rare mother-of-pearl
This beautiful, large, iridescent button dates from the 1950s and is made of especially thick mother-of-pearl. Such quality is seldom found these days.

Pearl-shell buttons with shanks
Self-shanks are made in one piece, with the shank cut out of the pearl. Chunky trochus is easier to find than suitable mother-of-pearl, which usually requires a separate shank, often made of metal.

Dark mother-of-pearl
Tahiti pearl, from Polynesia, has a rich, iridescent gray color that varies in depth. These striking buttons have been hand-milled to make them even more alluring.

Petal hand-cut from mother-of-pearl

Intricate latticework

Dyed abalone

Bee shape on trochus

Chamfered petal in trochus

Engraved and carved pearl shell
Delicate designs, from simple beveling to intricate floral themes, catch the light, trick the eye, and enhance the natural luster of these buttons.

Metal embellishment
From latticework to golden bees encased in polyester, metal and metallic effects offset the exquisite sheen of pearl to produce magnificent buttons.

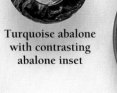

Turquoise abalone with contrasting abalone inset

Tahiti pearl-shell bar inlaid in heavy mother-of-pearl disk

Inlaid pearl
Various types of pearl shell can combine to contrast or tone with each other in simple and complex designs.

Inlaid pieces precision-cut to fit together like a jigsaw

Turban shells
These buttons are made from the operculum, or trapdoor, of the turban shell, which seals the aperture of the shell when the occupant withdraws inside.

Bold & Bright Buttons

When combined with vibrant summer cottons or bulky winter knitwear, these cheerful buttons make a strong statement. From fun flat shapes like tiddlywinks, to vivid blocks and marbles, they add a playful and entertaining note to any garment.

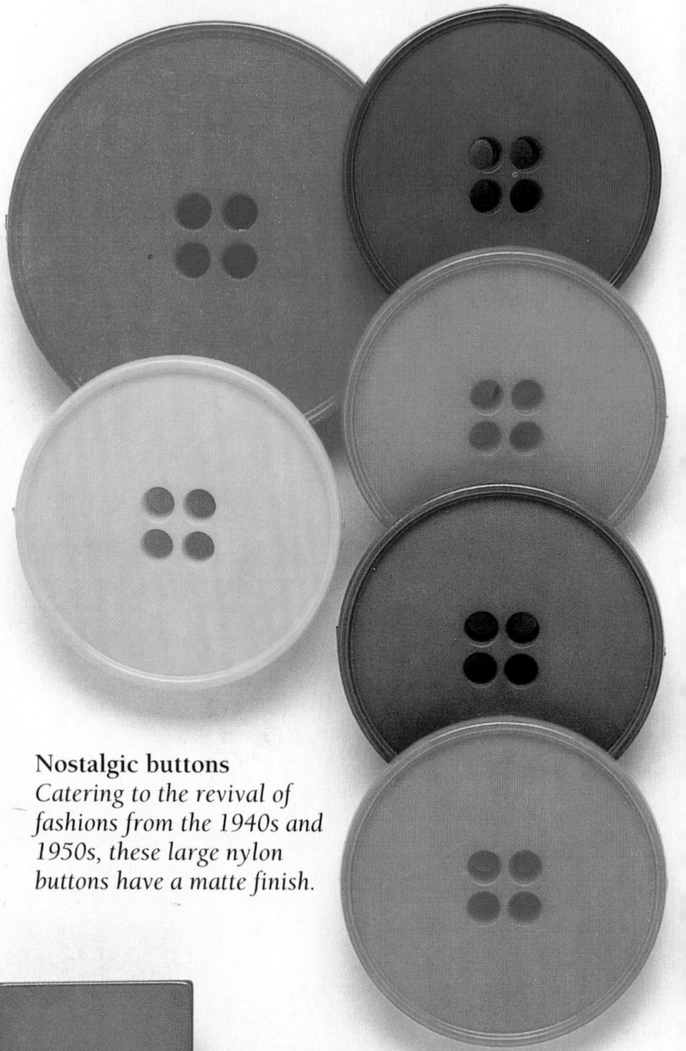

Domed buttons
These simple, glossy nylon buttons look particularly effective in a row of contrasting colors.

Nylon shank

Nostalgic buttons
Catering to the revival of fashions from the 1940s and 1950s, these large nylon buttons have a matte finish.

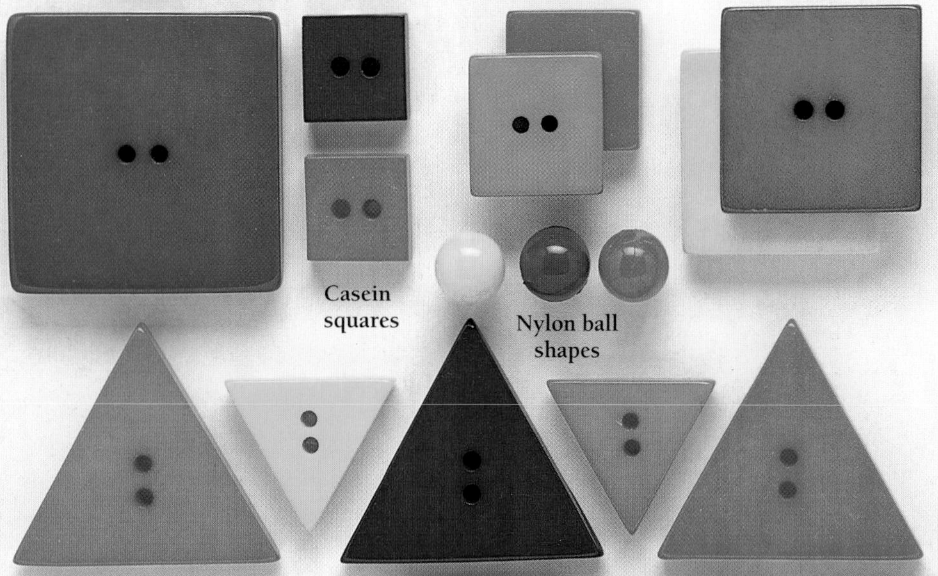

Casein squares

Nylon ball shapes

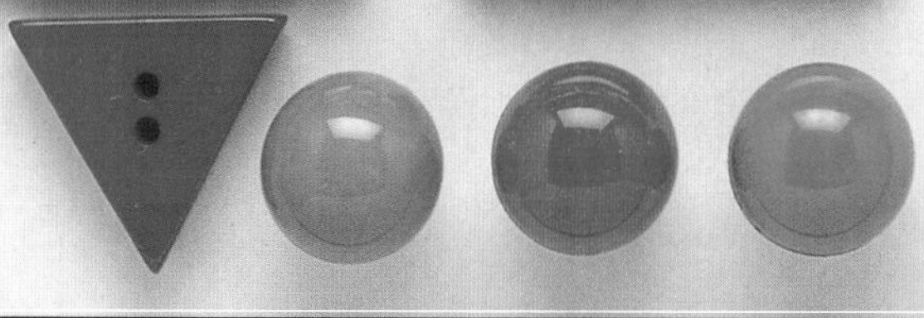

Flower shape cut from casein

Geometric shapes
Made of casein and nylon in a variety of shapes and sizes, these buttons introduce a sense of fun to any outfit.

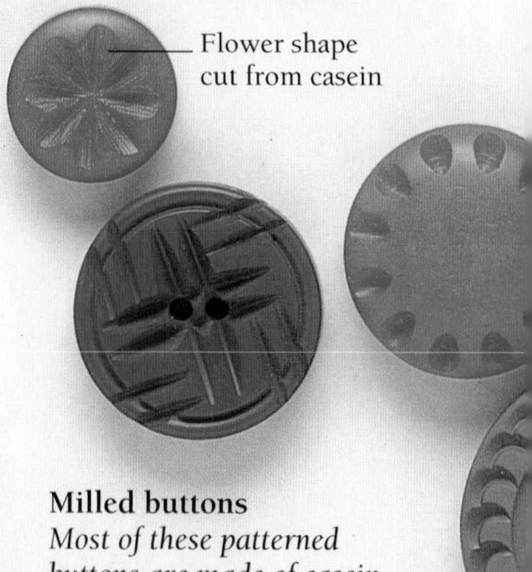

Milled buttons
Most of these patterned buttons are made of casein, a mixture of dried milk and a preservative, which is poured into trays and cut into blank disks once it has hardened. The buttons are milled before being dyed.

Novelty shapes
*These fun buttons are made
from nylon and casein.
Although casein has been
widely replaced by cheaper
plastics, it is still used to
produce high-quality hand-
worked buttons.*

**Metal
eyelet**

**Casein
toggle**

**Casein
daisy**

Nylon toggles

**Large 1940s triangle
cut from molded
sheet plastic**

**Milled surface
design**

Pearly luster
*Some plastics can be treated to provide
sheen, translucence, and pearl effects that
are gentler on the eye than solid color.*

Lozenge-shaped buttons
*Beveled edges on these
colored buttons provide a
three-dimensional effect and
enhance their unusual shapes.*

**Milled
casein**

A Delicate Effect

Though feminine and softly tinted, pastel buttons do not have to be insipid. Instead of consistently matching them with pale fabrics, try setting them off against black or other dark colors. Choose large buttons for extra impact, and experiment with different shapes.

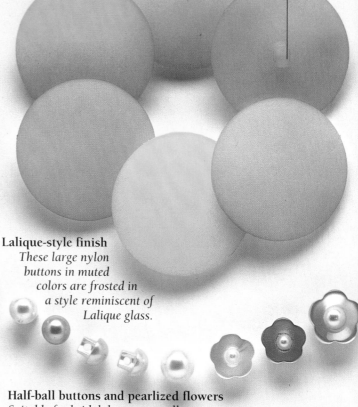

Molded nylon shank

Lightly textured flowers
Made in molds, these nylon flowers make colorful dress or shirt buttons.

Lalique-style finish
These large nylon buttons in muted colors are frosted in a style reminiscent of Lalique glass.

Lucite buttons
To make this unusual shape, round buttons are cut from a Lucite sheet and ground by hand on both sides with a V-shaped cutter.

Half-ball buttons and pearlized flowers
Suitable for bridal dresses as well as simpler clothes, the ball buttons are made of nylon, the flowers of polyester.

Polyester buttons
Coordinating pastel pearlized strips are captured within polyester and add texture.

Nylon roses
Molded nylon produces flowers with considerable detail in a variety of colors.

Fans and shells
Nylon lends itself to a wide range of shapes. These buttons offer a contrast to floral and geometric themes.

Etched and painted roses
Flowers are engraved and hand-painted on the back of these Lucite buttons, creating a three-dimensional effect in places the paint does not penetrate completely.

Etched area virtually untouched by paint

Clear buttons
Unusual shapes and delicate decoration enhance clear Lucite and glass buttons. Many imitation glass buttons are so convincing that only by touching them can you tell they are synthetic: glass is cold to the touch, synthetics are warm.

Translucent color
A touch of color provides a gentle effect in glass and synthetics. Different materials can be embedded within polyester to give color. Glass paperweight buttons are made over a flame from glass canes.

Herringbone pattern
in Lucite

Foil-backed
glass

Tinted
molded
glass

1930s pressed
glass

Colored flecks
encased in polyester

Hand-painted
Chinese-style
flowers on glass

Paperweight buttons

Gilded pressed
glass

Hand-painted
glass

Painted and printed buttons
Glass and nylon can be hand-painted or printed to produce particularly feminine buttons with floral themes.

Fabric roses
Satin ribbon is fashioned by hand into a rose with leaves, and a nylon shank is attached. These buttons complement embroidered cardigans.

Daisies
Solid-color nylon flowers in many different styles are produced in enormous quantities from injection molds.

Hearts and bows
Dainty shapes are ideal for decorating children's clothes.

Couturier Style

A few carefully chosen buttons can provide glamour and impact, giving an exclusive designer feel to a homemade or off-the-rack garment. Whether you want to create a bold, dramatic look or a restrained classic evening style, there is a wealth of textures and designs to choose from. Inexpensive copies are available, but for special occasions it is worth investing in genuine hand-finished buttons.

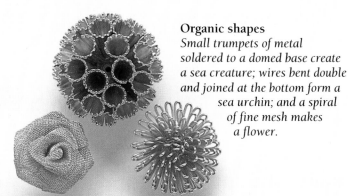

Organic shapes
Small trumpets of metal soldered to a domed base create a sea creature; wires bent double and joined at the bottom form a sea urchin; and a spiral of fine mesh makes a flower.

Metal filigree
set in casein

Cast metal filigree in old brass

Old and modern filigree
Special antique finishes, applied to modern metal buttons, make them barely distinguishable from older ones.

Decorative back of modern filigree button

Textured composition (a mixture of plastics)

Cabochon set in fabric-trimmed composition

A night at the theater
Looking as though they belong on sumptuous theater costumes, these buttons combine fabric with metal or plastic.

Velvet secured by decorative claws

Bead effect created in nylon

Beaded buttons
Beads add a distinctive touch to evening wear. They can be threaded and coiled over a mold or glued to a braid-covered button. Convincing copies of beaded buttons can be made from molded nylon.

Bugle-encrusted braid button

Spiraled fabric
Starting at the center, the fabric is wound around and secured with glue. Much skill is needed to make these handmade buttons.

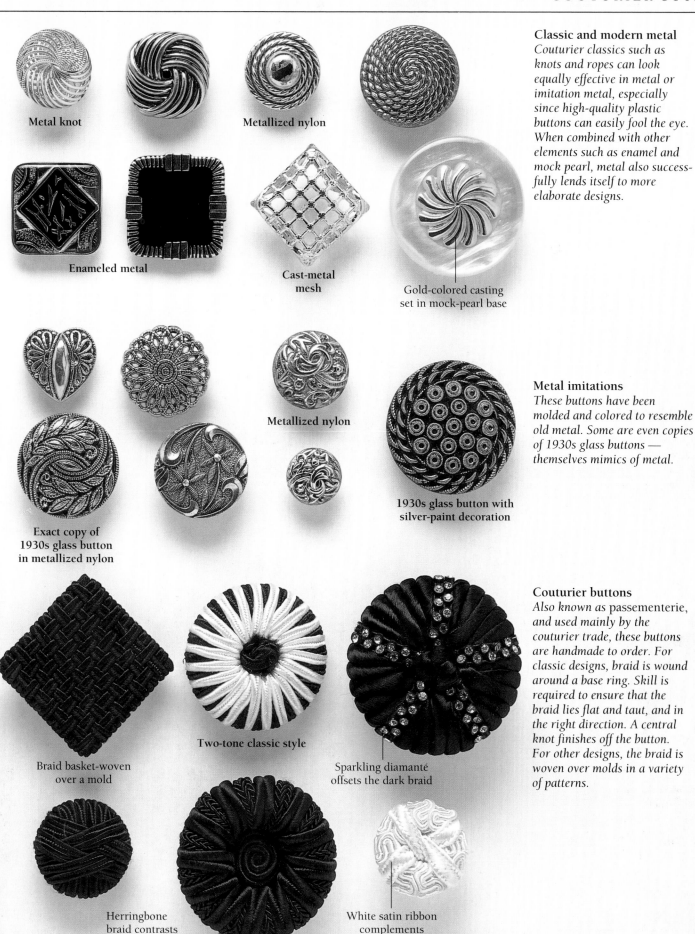

Metal knot

Metallized nylon

Enameled metal

Cast-metal mesh

Gold-colored casting set in mock-pearl base

Metallized nylon

1930s glass button with silver-paint decoration

Exact copy of 1930s glass button in metallized nylon

Braid basket-woven over a mold

Two-tone classic style

Sparkling diamanté offsets the dark braid

Herringbone braid contrasts with plain satin

White satin ribbon complements decorative braid

Classic and modern metal
Couturier classics such as knots and ropes can look equally effective in metal or imitation metal, especially since high-quality plastic buttons can easily fool the eye. When combined with other elements such as enamel and mock pearl, metal also success-fully lends itself to more elaborate designs.

Metal imitations
These buttons have been molded and colored to resemble old metal. Some are even copies of 1930s glass buttons — themselves mimics of metal.

Couturier buttons
Also known as passementerie, and used mainly by the couturier trade, these buttons are handmade to order. For classic designs, braid is wound around a base ring. Skill is required to ensure that the braid lies flat and taut, and in the right direction. A central knot finishes off the button. For other designs, the braid is woven over molds in a variety of patterns.

Antique Buttons

Beautiful old buttons can give a garment an antique feel and go perfectly with exquisite old lace and nostalgic clothes. They can be found in markets and secondhand shops. Antique buttons reveal a wealth of fashion, social, and manufacturing history, all of which can inspire people to collect them. When starting a collection, it is a good idea to concentrate on a particular theme or era. Mount the buttons and decorate with fashion engravings and general ephemera to reflect their period.

Scene from *Carmen*

St. George and
the dragon

Victorian picture buttons
Buttons portraying scenes from opera, mythology, history, and nursery rhymes were very popular with the Victorians; so were floral subjects.

Dutch silver
Of the highest quality, rare silver buttons such as this could be up to 2½ inches in diameter. They may have been used as currency by Dutch merchants and sailors in the seventeenth century.

Sporting buttons
Sets were originally hand-made in a variety of materials including silver, pearl, and enamel. These two-piece stamped-brass examples were manufactured in the early nineteenth century.

Dorset
thread

Fabric buttons
First popular in the 1600s, embroidered buttons survived the advent of machines in the mid-nineteenth century; not so the handmade Dorset thread buttons, which disappeared virtually overnight.

Enamel on pierced
gilt brass

Paste set
in silver

Fine spangled buttons
Polished facets of cut steel or lead crystal cut into gemstones were used in place of diamonds for a brilliant effect on court dress and evening wear. The disadvantage of steel was that it rusted easily, even from moisture on people's hands.

Rivet set in
pierced brass

Wedgwood and Jasperware
Classical white figures or heads were modeled separately and applied to a colored clay background. This style was much in vogue in the late eighteenth century, frequently mounted in silver, steel, or paste settings.

Pearl backing

Enamelwork
Powdered glass was fired at high temperatures onto a metal base to form a hard, glassy surface; wires, deep engraving, or firing at successively lower temperatures kept the colors separate.

Nineteenth- and twentieth- century enamel

Pierced and enameled button

Ceramic

Glass

Tahiti pearl center

Painted ceramic and glass
Floral designs — always popular on buttons — were hand-painted with overglaze colors or enamel paints, and then the buttons were fired again.

Art Nouveau
The Art Nouveau movement, which was in part a revolt against shoddy machine workmanship, produced beautifully crafted buttons. Sinuous forms were characteristic.

Brass overlay on abalone

Steel cup

Imitation gem

Pearl shell
Employed extensively in button-making during the 1800s, pearl shell was used on its own, elaborately cut and carved, or combined with metal and diamanté for more ornate buttons.

Gold and silver foil on Tahiti pearl

Pearl-shell background

Habitat buttons
Like miniature display cases, these eighteenth-century buttons contained grasses, shells, feathers, even insects.

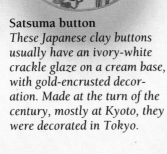

Satsuma button
These Japanese clay buttons usually have an ivory-white crackle glaze on a cream base, with gold-encrusted decoration. Made at the turn of the century, mostly at Kyoto, they were decorated in Tokyo.

Austrian tinies
Fashionable between 1890 and 1920, these two-piece metal buttons from Austria were worn in long rows on sleeves and bodices.

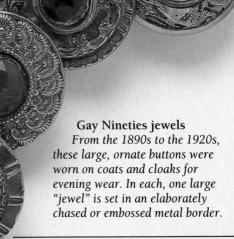

Gay Nineties jewels
From the 1890s to the 1920s, these large, ornate buttons were worn on coats and cloaks for evening wear. In each, one large "jewel" is set in an elaborately chased or embossed metal border.

Handmade Buttons

Distinctive hand-crafted buttons add an exclusive element to any outfit. They are produced in small numbers from a variety of materials, including ceramics, modeling clay, wood, and fabric; each button is individual. To avoid damaging them, remove handmade buttons from clothes before cleaning.

Woodland flowers
These buttons are made of modeling clay with an exceptionally intricate floral design.

Fine leaf detail

Ethnic style

Two-tone effect

Painted wood
These wooden buttons have been carved and painted. Varnish protects both the wood and the decoration.

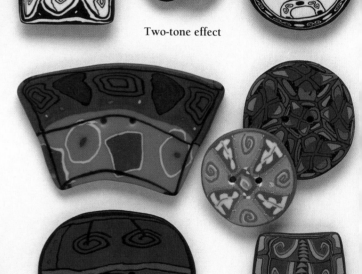

Metal shank attached before resin hardens

Embroidered buttons
Bold modern designs are available as well as more traditional themes.

Resin snails
Resin can be poured into a mold and given a metallic finish to produce shapes like these amusing snails.

Abstract designs in clay
Different colors of modeling clay are combined in elaborate designs to make these striking buttons.

Hand-painted novelties

Glazed pansy

Delicate transfer prints

Feathered marble look

Porcelain buttons
Dainty yet durable, porcelain can be used to make buttons in a wide range of styles, from printed flowers to naïve novelties.

Modern ceramics
The bold abstract designs on these glazed ceramic buttons evoke the 1960s and 1970s. The irregular shapes of the squares add to their charm.

Face made from two colors of clay

Green oxide applied to stoneware

Stoneware shank

Chinese and Celtic style
These earthenware and stoneware buttons are press-molded and glazed with mixtures of matte oxides.

Witty ceramics
These eye-catching ghosts and ghouls are fun for adults and children alike.

Novelty Buttons

Children love brightly colored buttons in a mixture of shapes and sizes, and will enjoy learning to fasten them. Choose from a wide variety of images — from miniature cars to chunky musical notes. Many novelties are even suitable for adults. For extra impact, try mixing shapes and colors within a theme: dress to impress with an environmental motif or a fruit-flavored flair. Remember that buttons can be used as decoration as well as for practical purposes. It is best, though, to avoid using dark buttons on light fabric, because the surface dye may rub off. For children's clothes, sew all buttons on securely to make sure youngsters cannot pull them off, and avoid glass buttons and shapes with sharp edges.

Molded shank

Going places
These buttons depicting various methods of transportation are made of molded nylon. All but the silver plane have been hand-painted in bold primaries for a naïve effect.

Metallized nylon

Simple shapes in modeling clay

Plated cast metal

Resin

Nylon

Picture buttons in modeling clay

Beside the sea
Perfect for summer clothing, these are made of various substances. The picture buttons are intricately crafted from modeling clay. Hand-wash clay buttons in luke-warm water or remove before cleaning.

Hand-painted nylon

Animals and pets
The pig's-head button is a slice from a roll of clay with the same pattern running all the way through. The ceramic buttons are handmade and durable.

Nylon

Modeling clay

Ceramic

Ceramic

Hand-painted design stamped onto wood

Teddy bears' picnic
Nylon, ceramic, and modeling clay combine in a favorite theme to create these friendly, cheerful buttons.

Animal farm
Try alternating these hand-painted animals, or simply vary the colors.

Christmas ornaments
Decorate a child's outfit for the holidays with Christmas buttons. Try making your own designs by applying enamel paint to a plain nylon button.

Nylon

Enameled metal

Enamel paint decoration

Modeling clay

Nylon

Flying fastenings
These buttons would look pretty on a dark fabric. The painted nylon lady-bugs are easy to fasten.

33

Novelty Buttons

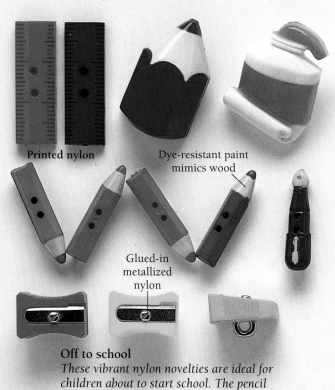

Printed nylon

Dye-resistant paint mimics wood

Glued-in metallized nylon

Off to school
These vibrant nylon novelties are ideal for children about to start school. The pencil sharpeners are made with a pretend blade.

At home
People buttons come in various shapes and occupations. Any child will enjoy choosing the house to go with each character.

Modeling clay

Nylon

Resin

Nylon

Celestial buttons
Moon and star buttons look great on dark fabrics, while the unusual sun made of resin would suit children's and adults' clothes alike. For young children, it is best to avoid sharp edges and points.

Flower power
Big, bold nylon flowers make colorful coat buttons. A row of cheerful bees could brighten a plain shirt.

Alphabet set
Bright letters and numbers can make spelling and counting more fun. For safety reasons, always avoid spelling a child's name on his or her clothing.

Hands and feet
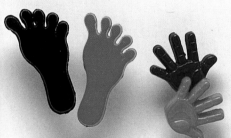
These amusing buttons look effective in a row of different colors, sewn on at different angles.

Wooden dice
These are made of wood sprayed with color. The spots have been painted on by hand.

Making time
Beautifully detailed, these clocks have an old-fashioned charm about them. The glass ones, though, are suitable only for adults.

Printed metal with
clear resin finish
resembling glass

Molded glass with
hand-painted numerals

Made in
two parts

Striking a note
Make a statement with big chunky notes, miniature records, or a curvy piano — all in molded nylon. For a more discreet look, choose smaller versions, or buttons like this violin and saxophone.

Metallized nylon

Two pieces
clicked together

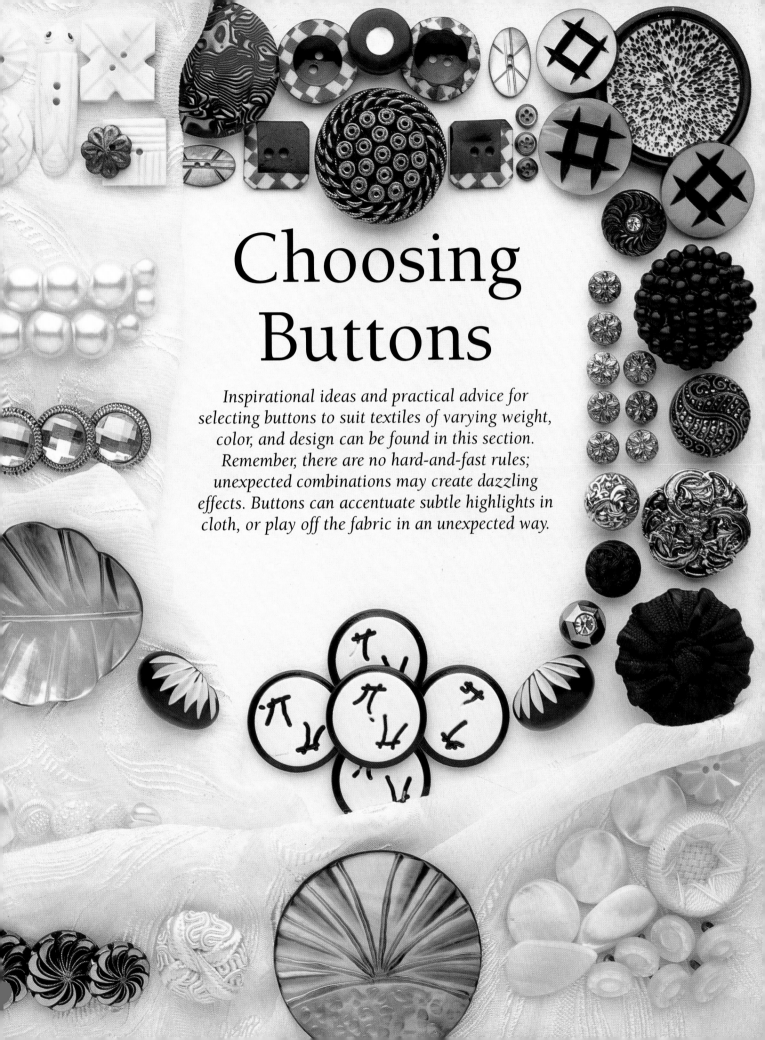

Choosing Buttons

Inspirational ideas and practical advice for selecting buttons to suit textiles of varying weight, color, and design can be found in this section. Remember, there are no hard-and-fast rules; unexpected combinations may create dazzling effects. Buttons can accentuate subtle highlights in cloth, or play off the fabric in an unexpected way.

Reds & Browns

Complement the spicy warm tones of reds, golds, and browns with buttons of matching hues or metallic finishes to create a rich sensuous mood. Depending on their pattern and style, gold and bronze finishes are suitable for a daytime or evening look; multicolor buttons can be chosen either to blend or to make a bold statement.

Antique-brass finish
Contrasting with the highly decorative fabric, these simple buttons provide a practical look.

Fine Indian silk seersucker

Two-tone translucent buttons
The different colors in the fabric show through these buttons for a rich effect.

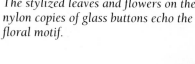

Metal-look buttons
The stylized leaves and flowers on these nylon copies of glass buttons echo the floral motif.

Pearl-effect buttons
Sumptuous black-rimmed polyester buttons in dark red complement the two-tone effect.

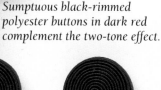

A large cameo button can be worn at the neck like a brooch

Spiral fabric buttons
Reminiscent of the fifties, small black braid buttons add a touch of nostalgic elegance.

Printed cotton

Speckled buttons
The dark flecks on these ruby red buttons contrast boldly with the pattern.

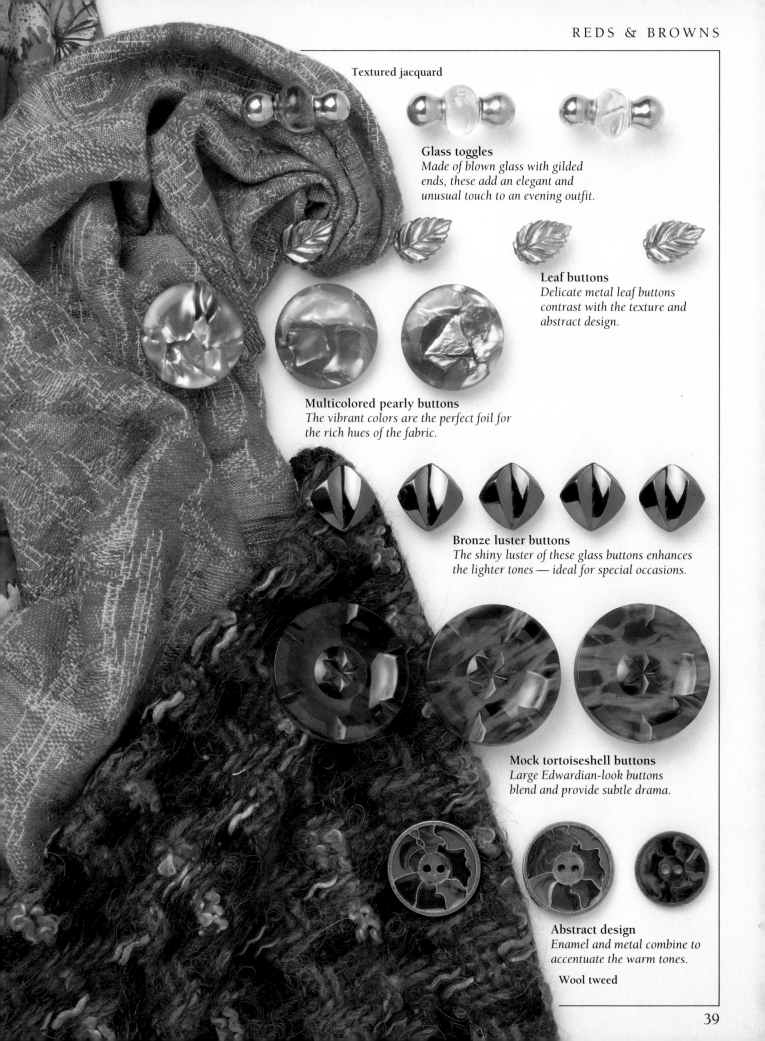

Textured jacquard

Glass toggles
Made of blown glass with gilded ends, these add an elegant and unusual touch to an evening outfit.

Leaf buttons
Delicate metal leaf buttons contrast with the texture and abstract design.

Multicolored pearly buttons
The vibrant colors are the perfect foil for the rich hues of the fabric.

Bronze luster buttons
The shiny luster of these glass buttons enhances the lighter tones — ideal for special occasions.

Mock tortoiseshell buttons
Large Edwardian-look buttons blend and provide subtle drama.

Abstract design
Enamel and metal combine to accentuate the warm tones.

Wool tweed

Blues & Greens

Fabrics in shades ranging from deep sea green to pale lilac blend naturally with the iridescent hues of lustrous buttons. They also suit the jewel-like colors of glass, and the sheen of pearl and enamel. Select buttons to match the texture of a fabric or highlight a motif, choosing buttons in a darker shade for a strong, sumptuous effect.

Delicate silk chiffon

Dyed mother-of-pearl buttons
These beveled buttons change color as they catch the light, echoing the sheen of the fabric.

Blue glass buttons
The black design circling the button gives a Tyrolean feel.

Molded buttons
Made from glass decorated in silver and blue, these buttons are ideal for a special evening.

Millefiori buttons
Dark blue floral buttons, forged from slices of molten glass canes, look strong against pale fabric.

Bright buttons
Effective run in pairs or threes, these glass buttons pick up the turquoise stripe.

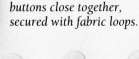

Pewter look
Use these heavy-looking buttons close together, secured with fabric loops.

A shimmering luster button creates a bold feature at neck or shoulder

Transparent flowers
The palest lilac floral buttons, highlighted with diamanté, complete a light floating evening dress.

Raw silk

Brocade

Marbleized buttons
The rich colors and sheen of these gold-veined buttons suggest a Renaissance theme.

Silver foliage buttons
Ornate but refined, these heavy silver buttons in Art Nouveau style complement the weighty splendor of the brocade.

Blue rope buttons
With a luster finish, these beaded ropelike twists highlight the fabric's sophisticated pattern.

Classic daytime buttons
Plain yet elegant, these classic gold-edged buttons would look handsome on a jacket.

Paisley buttons
Edged with a peacock-green rope effect, these buttons have a sumptuous feel.

Foil-backed glass
With their iridescent colors, reminiscent of an exotic bird's wing, these buttons look striking on rich velvet.

Cotton velvet

Pastels

Pastel colors need not be merely pretty, delicate, and feminine. Depending on the choice of buttons, they can be vibrant and exciting, or crisply elegant. Changing buttons each season will transform a wardrobe to mirror fresh innovations in fashion.

Luster buttons
Sparkling glass highlights the soft pinks in the fabric.

Mirror bows
Made from lightweight nylon, these pale green buttons look stunning on special occasions.

Fine Swiss cotton

1930s mother-of-pearl buttons
Dyed pink, these shimmering cut ovals have a delicate appeal on patterned fabric.

Buttons for daytime
Petals cut from the reverse of a green-backed shell accentuate the yellow tones.

Speckled buttons
Glittering plastic has a transparent quality that suits lightweight fabric.

Matte pastel bows
Matching the dots with alternate-colored bows creates a strong effect for day wear.

Pearlized dome-shaped buttons
Draw attention to the pink tones with shiny pearls, perfect for weddings.

Cotton lawn

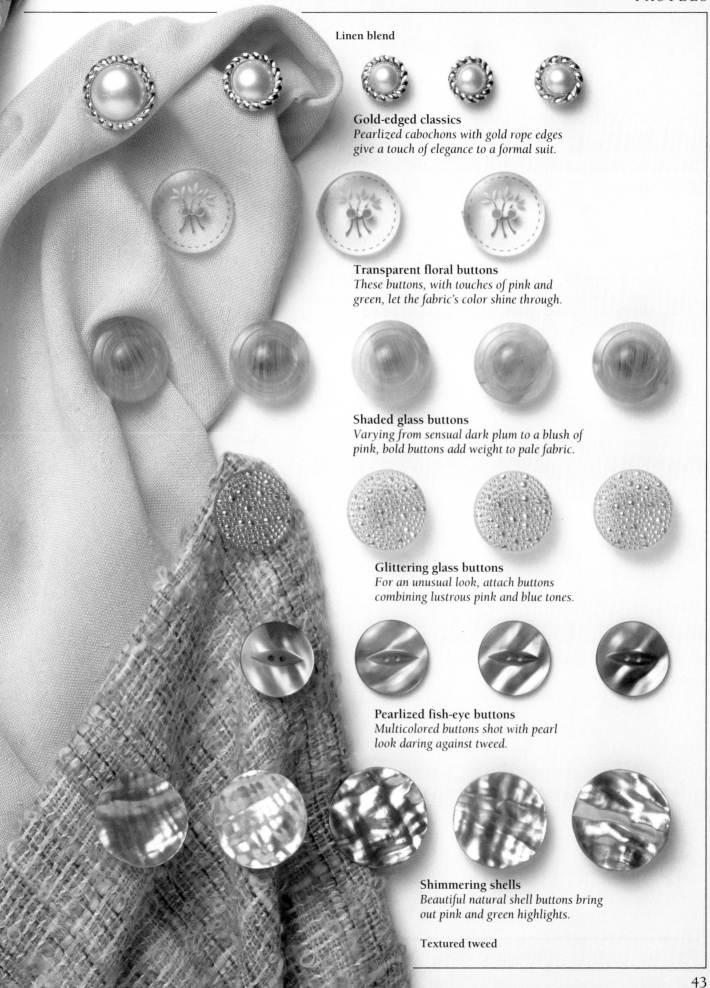

Linen blend

Gold-edged classics
Pearlized cabochons with gold rope edges give a touch of elegance to a formal suit.

Transparent floral buttons
These buttons, with touches of pink and green, let the fabric's color shine through.

Shaded glass buttons
Varying from sensual dark plum to a blush of pink, bold buttons add weight to pale fabric.

Glittering glass buttons
For an unusual look, attach buttons combining lustrous pink and blue tones.

Pearlized fish-eye buttons
Multicolored buttons shot with pearl look daring against tweed.

Shimmering shells
Beautiful natural shell buttons bring out pink and green highlights.

Textured tweed

Black & White

Black and white can look sharp, sleek, and dramatic, or subtle and sophisticated. Select buttons to accentuate the effect you want by looking at the texture, color, and pattern of the fabric, and notice, too, the way it catches the light. Pearlized and metallic buttons are particularly effective against silky grays and creams, while metal and horn finishes complement tweedy fabrics.

Glittering gray buttons
Shiny hematite, framed with diamanté, picks out the silver tones in the glamorous fabric.

Tiger-eye stripe
These gold-rimmed glass buttons add a modern touch.

Fine silk voile

Metallized silver buttons
The Norwegian style adds a formal note to a tailored outfit.

Art Deco design
Square two-tone buttons have a bold geometric style.

Delicate embossed buttons
Touched with a hint of gold, white glass gives an 18th-century look.

Glass blouse buttons
The ridged motif echoes the embroidery on the fabric.

Large pearlized globes
Rows of shimmering balls look stunning on a loose blouse.

Silk acetate

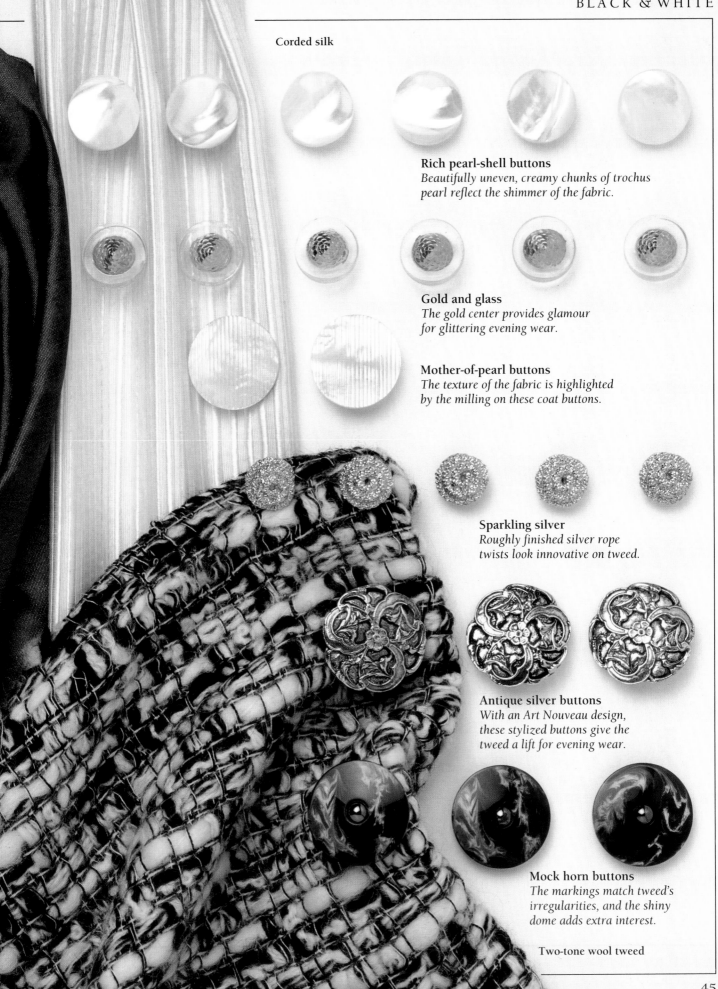

Corded silk

Rich pearl-shell buttons
Beautifully uneven, creamy chunks of trochus pearl reflect the shimmer of the fabric.

Gold and glass
The gold center provides glamour for glittering evening wear.

Mother-of-pearl buttons
The texture of the fabric is highlighted by the milling on these coat buttons.

Sparkling silver
Roughly finished silver rope twists look innovative on tweed.

Antique silver buttons
With an Art Nouveau design, these stylized buttons give the tweed a lift for evening wear.

Mock horn buttons
The markings match tweed's irregularities, and the shiny dome adds extra interest.

Two-tone wool tweed

Patterned Fabrics

Although classic plain buttons can look stylish on patterned fabrics, they should be a first choice rather than a last resort. An imaginatively chosen fancy button can transform homemade garments into designer wear. Study the shapes or motifs in the fabric, and decide on the colors you wish to emphasize.

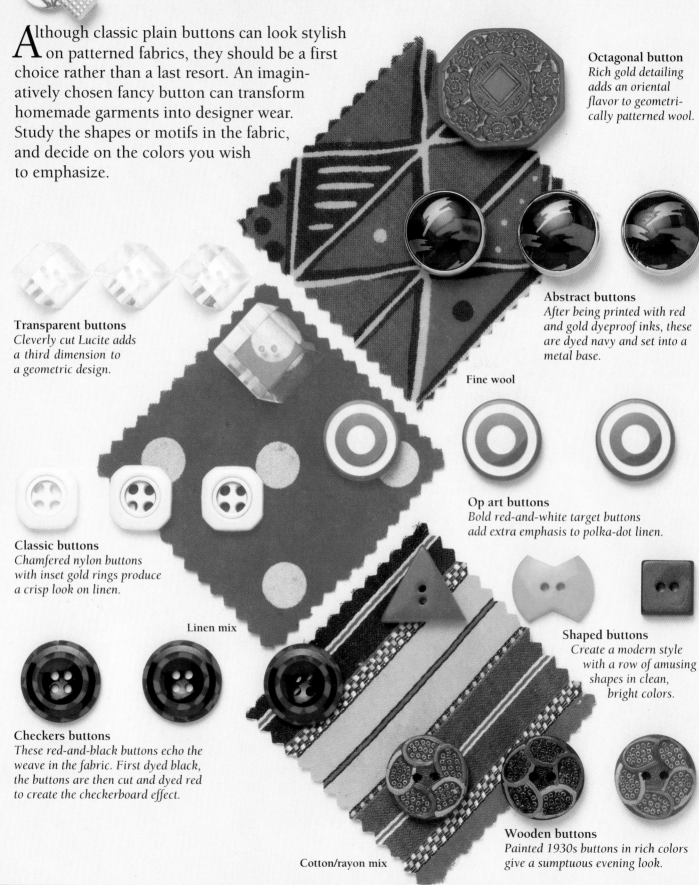

Octagonal button
Rich gold detailing adds an oriental flavor to geometrically patterned wool.

Abstract buttons
After being printed with red and gold dyeproof inks, these are dyed navy and set into a metal base.

Fine wool

Transparent buttons
Cleverly cut Lucite adds a third dimension to a geometric design.

Op art buttons
Bold red-and-white target buttons add extra emphasis to polka-dot linen.

Classic buttons
Chamfered nylon buttons with inset gold rings produce a crisp look on linen.

Linen mix

Shaped buttons
Create a modern style with a row of amusing shapes in clean, bright colors.

Checkers buttons
These red-and-black buttons echo the weave in the fabric. First dyed black, the buttons are then cut and dyed red to create the checkerboard effect.

Wooden buttons
Painted 1930s buttons in rich colors give a sumptuous evening look.

Cotton/rayon mix

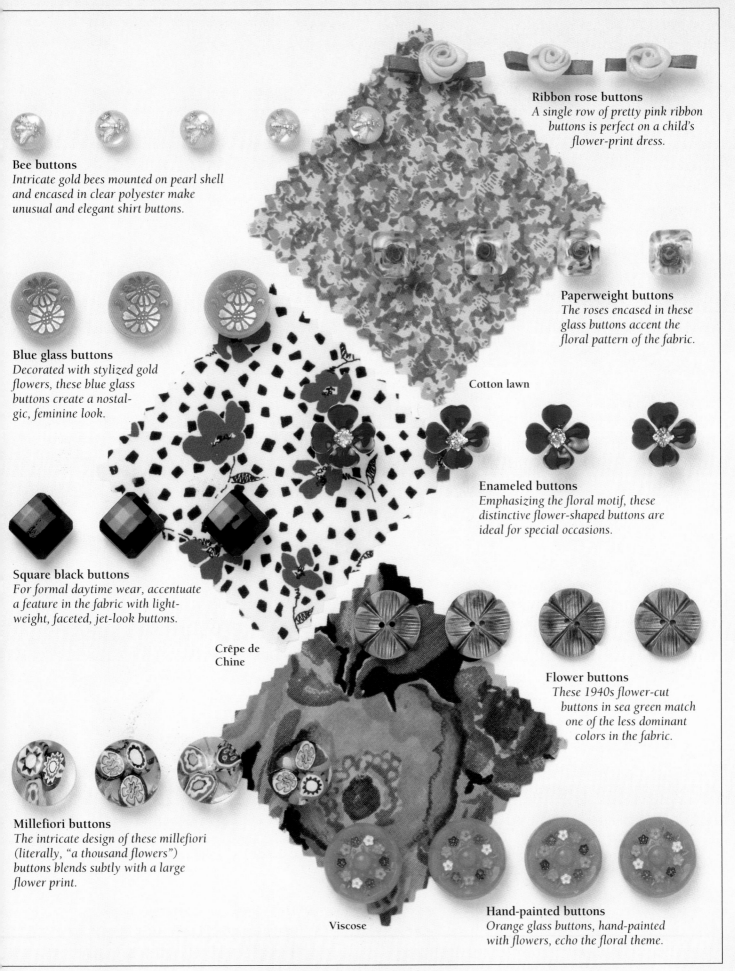

Ribbon rose buttons
A single row of pretty pink ribbon buttons is perfect on a child's flower-print dress.

Bee buttons
Intricate gold bees mounted on pearl shell and encased in clear polyester make unusual and elegant shirt buttons.

Paperweight buttons
The roses encased in these glass buttons accent the floral pattern of the fabric.

Blue glass buttons
Decorated with stylized gold flowers, these blue glass buttons create a nostalgic, feminine look.

Cotton lawn

Enameled buttons
Emphasizing the floral motif, these distinctive flower-shaped buttons are ideal for special occasions.

Square black buttons
For formal daytime wear, accentuate a feature in the fabric with lightweight, faceted, jet-look buttons.

Crêpe de Chine

Flower buttons
These 1940s flower-cut buttons in sea green match one of the less dominant colors in the fabric.

Millefiori buttons
The intricate design of these millefiori (literally, "a thousand flowers") buttons blends subtly with a large flower print.

Viscose

Hand-painted buttons
Orange glass buttons, hand-painted with flowers, echo the floral theme.

Knitting Yarns

Whe choosing buttons for yarn, it is always advisable to look at a small knitted sample first, since every yarn knits up differently. Textures and patterns become apparent and random colors become more, or less, pronounced than expected. Select buttons that suit the weight of the yarn, although the buttonholes can be altered to accommodate different sizes.

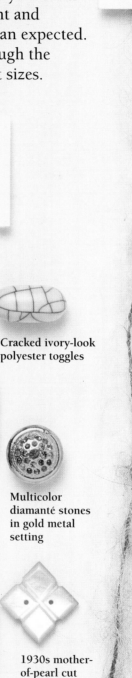

Pearly bow-shaped buttons

Enameled buttons

Mirrored button made with printed foil backing

Shell button

Dyed clear nylon buttons

Abalone shell

Metal Art Nouveau style

Cracked ivory-look polyester toggles

Multicolor diamanté stones in gold metal setting

1930s mother-of-pearl cut squares

Cotton
Perfect for summer wear, cotton yarn knits up to make a matte-finished, firm-textured garment. It can be plain in texture or have cablework and detailed patterning, so choose either a simple color-matched button or a more decorative button to complement the pattern.

Silk
Silk yarn has a sleek lustrous texture in a finished garment. Here, random dyeing gives it a bold splash of color. Mother-of-pearl complements the sheen, while a textured cream button can look stylish, and sparkling diamanté elegant.

Mohair
Depending on the style of button chosen, mohair can be made to look smart and feminine, or warm and simple. It knits up into a fluffy, loose weave that is substantial enough to take reasonably large buttons.

Iridescent glass
buttons

Dyed wooden
toggles

1930s toggle with
leaf pattern cut
into ends

Curved dyed
shell buttons

Handmade
modeling-
clay buttons

Cut natural pearl-
shell buttons

Matte-finished
double-dyed
nylon button

Wooden dome
hand-painted with
flecks of color

Casein, dyed
and burned for
a natural look

Velvet in old
gold-tone metal

Iridescent
textured glass

Art Deco button
in early plastic

Chenille
Heavy and suitable for softly draped styles, chenille knits up to make a firm but fairly open-weave garment. Its rich, velvety texture makes it perfect for evening wear, when dramatic buttons can be used to tremendous effect.

Shetland
Dotted with tiny flecks of color, this versatile Shetland yarn knits up to a very firm texture. It can be made into a multitude of styles, and each one can be enhanced by imaginatively chosen buttons.

Jacob wool
Thick, chunky, hand-spun Jacob wool yarn turns into big, natural-looking, dramatic garments. Choose buttons to bring out the bold look or to blend subtly with the variegated, twisted yarn.

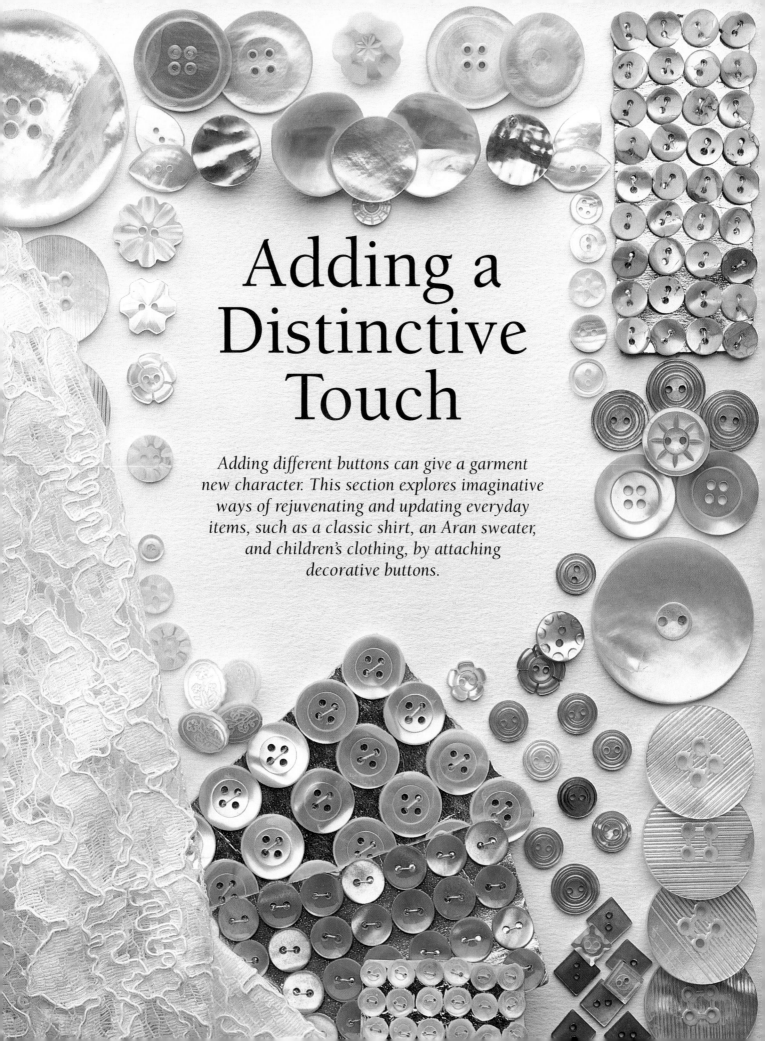

Adding a
Distinctive
Touch

*Adding different buttons can give a garment
new character. This section explores imaginative
ways of rejuvenating and updating everyday
items, such as a classic shirt, an Aran sweater,
and children's clothing, by attaching
decorative buttons.*

Styling a Jacket

Used as accessories, buttons can transform a classic summer or winter jacket and instantly tie it in with the rest of your outfit for either day or evening wear. Although a black jacket is an obvious choice for evenings, the appropriate buttons can add sophistication to a light one, too. For a really versatile garment, change the buttons for different occasions.

Jackets with original buttons

LOOKS FOR A LIGHT JACKET

LOOKS FOR A DARK JACKET

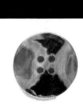

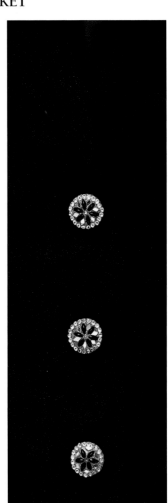

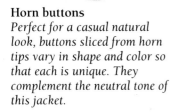

Horn buttons
Perfect for a casual natural look, buttons sliced from horn tips vary in shape and color so that each is unique. They complement the neutral tone of this jacket.

Twenties-style buttons
Create a nostalgic evening look with these intricate embossed and enameled metal buttons. They would complement a sumptuous outfit of patterned chiffon, velvet, or silk.

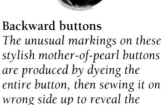

Backward buttons
The unusual markings on these stylish mother-of-pearl buttons are produced by dyeing the entire button, then sewing it on wrong side up to reveal the pattern of the shell.

Decorative Indian buttons
Beads and tiny reflective pieces of glass in resin give these buttons a sparkling 1960s ethnic effect. This look would tie in with bright colors and plenty of jewelry.

Inscribed pearl buttons
Chinese in style, these intricately carved
Tahiti pearl buttons add an exotic hint to
day or evening wear. The effect is enhanced
here by the addition of a flower-shaped
mother-of-pearl brooch in a similar
color, made from a large button
(see instructions below).

TURNING A BUTTON INTO A BROOCH

A large decorative button with a shank can easily
be adapted to make a striking brooch. With the
help of an ordinary stickpin you can fasten the
button securely without permanently altering or
damaging it.

1 Put the button face down
on a flat surface and push
a stickpin through the shank
as far as it will go. You may
need to experiment with
pins of different sizes to ensure that the button lies flat
once it is in place.

2 Position the button on
the garment and push
the pin through the fabric —
first to the back, then return
it to the front, and through
again to the back. Check
that the pin is still pressed
through the shank as far as
it will go.

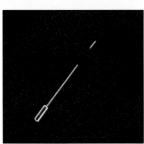

3 To finish, attach the cap
to the pin on the back of
the fabric so that it does not
show. Check that the button
is lying straight on the fabric
and make any minor adjust-
ments necessary.

Styling a Shirt

Buy an inexpensive classic shirt and jazz it up with a new set of buttons. Whether the top is worn loose and baggy over leggings, or trim and tucked into a tailored skirt, these small-scale fastenings can transform a wardrobe basic into something special. And it's easy to change the mood of your outfit in seconds with the button-changing technique described here.

Shirt with original buttons

Pearl-shell buttons
A rainbow of colors in mother-of-pearl adds interest to the neutral cream-colored shirt.

Bow-tie buttons
Try pearly bow-shaped buttons for an amusing effect. They look stylish but relaxed, especially when worn with a real bow tie for a whimsical touch.

Special occasion buttons
A quirky button can be worn for day or evening wear. These metal masks would be ideal for a theater trip. Choose appropriate buttons for different occasions.

Gleaming evening wear
Create an elegant look simply by putting a set of glittering crystal buttons down the front of a classic shirt, transforming it from a day shirt into perfect evening attire. Glass jet buttons would be an equally appropriate choice for a night on the town.

BUTTONS ON A STRIP

This cunning method of attaching different buttons means you can change styles as often as you like with a minimum of effort, and with hardly any sewing. First, remove the existing buttons and replace them with a second set of buttonholes exactly opposite the original holes.

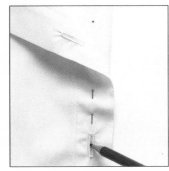

1 Cut a piece of fabric tape to fit the new buttonhole band. Finish the ends. Pin the tape beneath the band; mark the button positions through the holes with tailor's chalk or a pencil.

2 Remove the tape and sew the buttons onto it. (Using other pieces of tape, you can make as many different button strips as you like for both the shirtfront and the cuffs.)

3 Attach the button strip through either buttonhole band, depending on whether you want to fasten the shirt on the men's side or the women's side. Then button up as usual.

Styling Knitwear

Hand-knitted garments and machine-made woolens offer different criteria for button choices. The selection for a plain store-bought item is limited only by the size of the existing button-holes; the buttons can coordinate with accessories and be as decorative as you like. A handknit offers opportunities for matching intrinsic patterns and textures with different sizes of buttons.

Cardigans with original buttons

MACHINE-MADE GARMENT

HAND-KNITTED GARMENT

Glass millefiori
This dramatic millefiori button, made in the traditional Venetian method, would team well with a formal black skirt for day wear, or with black velvet and satin for evenings.

Gold roses
Delicate gold-plated ball buttons such as these are elegant for day or evening wear. Made of nylon, they are also light enough to sit comfortably on fine wool.

Red leather buttons
Traditional big Aran-style buttons covered in glossy red leather create an eye-catching variation on a theme and add warmth to the cream tones.

Filigree buttons
Intricately cut, domed silver filigree buttons reflect the elaborate textured patterns of an Aran cardigan and give it a stylish feminine look.

Creative buttons
Using leftover strands of wool, design your own buttons to match or contrast with a favorite handknit.

CREATIVE BUTTONS

Once you have mastered the basic techniques of using a creative button frame, let your imagination run wild. There is no limit to the variety of styles that you can design and the colors you can use if you think creatively.

1 Thread a darning needle with a piece of yarn, and bring it through the center of the button, leaving a long end of yarn on the underside. Then work the yarn from the center of the button around the inner rim to make a star shape.

2 Add a second color, this time starting on the outer rim. Leave a long end of yarn on the underside again. Fill in the border around the star completely.

3 Thread a third color through the center from the back, tie a loose knot, and thread the yarn back through the center. Pull tight to make a neat knot. Tie the loose ends, snip them short, and work them to the back of the button.

Reflecting a Style

Although fabric and style are usually the dressmaker's first choices, a particularly striking or unusual set of buttons could dictate the design of the garment you choose to make. The four very different looks shown here, made of exactly the same material, illustrate how different buttons can suggest contrasting styles, from tailored or geometric shirts to revealing evening wear or a feminine blouse.

Tailored look
Formal buttons are a natural foil for the clean lines of this restrained and elegant double-breasted style. The simple, classic design of these antique gold buttons, with twisted rope decoration around the rim, complements the look perfectly.

Geometric style
Shiny tin triangles suggest a trendy space-age or movie-usher look, especially when sewn on in the style of a uniform, as shown here. Other bold geometric shapes and large, military-style brass buttons would be equally appropriate.

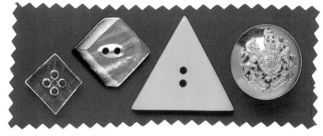

Other alternatives
Pearl and gold metal; satin gold metal; pearl; enameled center with brass rim.

Other alternatives
Square Lucite; plastic cube; casein triangle; crested brass.

HEAVY BUTTONS

Backing buttons and a stiffened button band make it possible to use heavy buttons on lightweight fabric. Often used by tailors, backing buttons prevent damage to fabric by holding the weight of a button. They are also ideal for leather.

1 Reinforce the button band by ironing fusible interfacing to the reverse side of the facing. Machine-sew the facing to the garment front.

2 Turn to the right side and press. Overlay the buttonhole band and mark where the buttons will go. Position the first decorative button.

3 Attach the button by sewing through the fabric to a backing button on the reverse.

Evening wear
A long row of large, iridescent glass buttons with faceted backs looks stunning for evenings or special occasions. Though heavy for lightweight fabric, they can be attached with a backing button to prevent pulling (see above).

Feminine look
These pierced pearl-shell buttons in a delicate flower shape accent a soft feminine style. The petals echo the scalloped neckline and button band, an effect that is highlighted here by the contrast in color between the buttons and the fabric.

Other alternatives
Diamanté flower; jewel button; lustered glass; diamanté in textured gold metal.

Other alternatives
Millefiori glass; iridescent glass heart; gold-mesh rose; glass paperweight button.

Fun Clothes for Children

Brightly colored novelty buttons make it easy to liven up toddlers' clothes. Eye-catching shapes, from cuddly teddies to lime green frogs, combine the decorative with the practical — and children quickly learn to fasten attractive buttons. With a little imagination and very little effort, you can transform ordinary playclothes into works of art.

Animal overalls
Large yellow teddy bears fasten these bright overalls, while multicolored fish swim along the waist and a procession of animals follows a front seam.

Colored clock T-shirt
For a T-shirt, use a simple image like this clockface, made up of bright numbers and tiny hands. The motif is echoed by stopwatches at the shoulder.

Hat and glove set
Help your child distinguish between left and right with glove buttons in different colors. Attach the buttons securely so they cannot be chewed off.

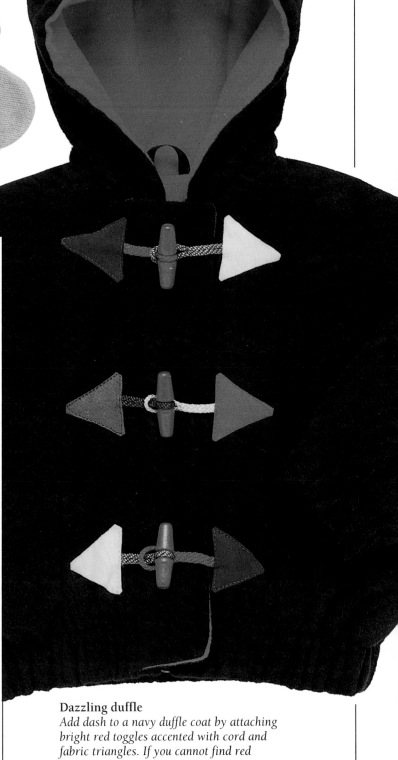

SEWING ON TOGGLES

Toggles are easy to attach and fun for children to use. Try wooden toggles, silky cord, and sturdy cotton twill in vibrant colors to make youngsters look forward to wearing a warm winter coat.

1 Cut a triangle from the cotton twill. Fold the edges over and tack. Place a piece of cord in a contrasting color around a toggle and then cross-stitch the length of the cord at the back to keep the two pieces together.

2 Position the toggle on the jacket and attach firmly by stitching over one end of the cord.

3 Place the triangle over the end of the cord and sew on all sides. Remove tacking. Using cord and twill in contrasting primaries, make a loop fastening on the other side of the coat.

Dazzling duffle
Add dash to a navy duffle coat by attaching bright red toggles accented with cord and fabric triangles. If you cannot find red toggles, paint natural wooden ones with several coats of nontoxic red wood stain.

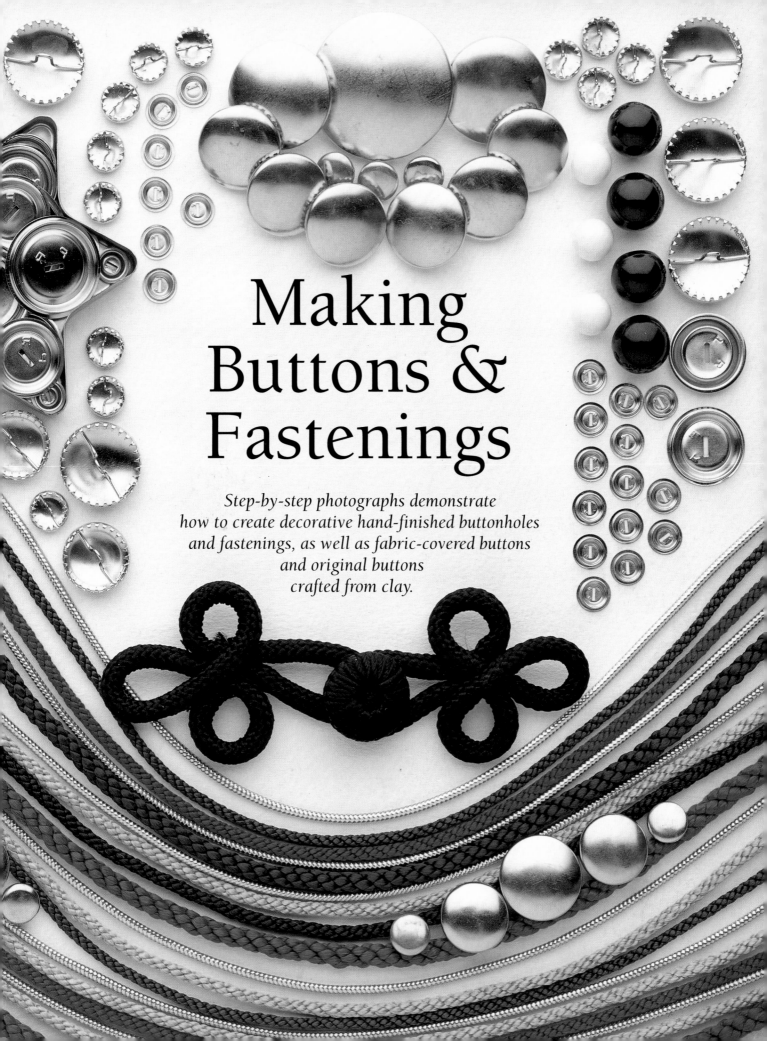

Making Buttons & Fastenings

*Step-by-step photographs demonstrate
how to create decorative hand-finished buttonholes
and fastenings, as well as fabric-covered buttons
and original buttons
crafted from clay.*

Hand-finished Buttonholes

Buttonholes worked or finished by hand give any garment a professional finish and, contrary to popular belief, are easy to make. Once the basic techniques are mastered, it is simple to incorporate decorative touches or to turn the buttonhole itself into an ornament. For knitted buttonholes, adapt the ideas shown here, using thick embroidery yarns.

BOUND BUTTONHOLE

Bound buttonholes add a tailor-made quality to a jacket, coat, or suit. Since the only hand-sewing involved is on the reverse of the garment, this method produces a neat buttonhole. Vary the effect by cutting the binding patch on a diagonal, as shown here, or make it a different color to match lapels and cuffs. As with most buttonholes, this type is made before assembling a garment.

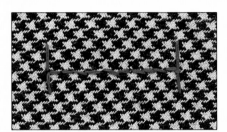

1 Mark the length of the button on the right side of the interfaced button band. Tack a fabric patch wrong side up exactly over the position line. The patch must be at least 1½ in wider than the buttonhole all around, depending on the fabric's weight and weave.

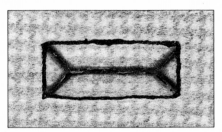

2 On the interfaced wrong side of the garment, machine-sew a rectangle of tiny firm stitches around the tacked position line, making sharp reinforced corners. Mark inside the rectangle as shown and cut along the lines; avoid snipping stitches at corners.

3 Ease the patch through the slit to the wrong side. Press each side away from the hole (it will not lie totally flat). This brings the seam allowances away from the opening.

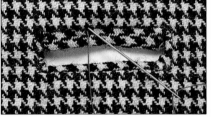

4 On the right side, form a buttonhole lip by rolling one long side into the middle, securing with stitches into the seam join. Repeat for the other lip so that the two meet in the middle. Press.

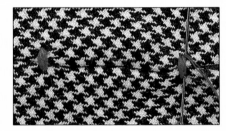

5 On the wrong side, press the folds made by forming the lips. Oversew the folds together at each end of the buttonhole with several stitches.

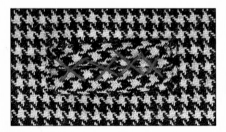

6 On the right side, tack the lips together and keep the tacking in until the garment is completed. This will prevent the buttonhole from being pulled out of shape.

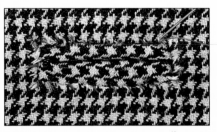

7 Finish the buttonhole at the back once the facing is added. For fraying or thick fabric, cut the slit in the facing as for step **2** to make good turnings. (For thin, firm fabrics, a simple slit is enough.) Roll the edges inward and hem.

8 Once the garment is completed, remove the tacking from the right side of the buttonhole and press flat.

HAND-SEWN BUTTONHOLE

The method shown here is used on men's suits to give an expensive hand-finished look. For a blouse or dress, the buttonhole slit is straight and no gimp is needed. Use buttonhole thread or twist that is slightly paler than the fabric; it will appear darker when seen *en masse*.

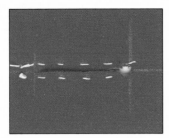

1 Mark the site and length of the buttonhole on the right side of the interfaced garment, and cut the slit. (Tailors use a special device to cut the shape shown here, but the round end can be made with a hole punch.)

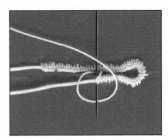

2 With sufficient thread for the entire buttonhole, work around using a blanket stitch. Sew over the gimp if using.

3 Make a bar across the straight end with three or four stitches side by side; work over them in blanket stitch. Finish with a neat knot on the wrong side and run the thread through a few stitches.

ROSE AND LEAVES

Simple nylon rose buttons and imaginatively embroidered leaf buttonholes create a striking decoration down the front of a blouse. Buttons and embroidery can be employed in an infinite variety of designs, both delicate and bold. For a strong effect, try wool on thick fabrics. In this example, embroidery thread is used, worked in satin and backstitch.

1 On the right side, measure the slit and machine-sew around it. Lightly pencil in the stalks and leaves. Cut the slit.

2 Buttonhole around the slit, embroidering the leaves and stalks as they come. Take the thread back to the wrong side before buttonholing again.

3 Finish off with a neat knot on the wrong side and run the thread through a few stitches. Check the final result with the button.

CAT ON A MAT

Combining a reversed bound buttonhole and a novelty button, this witty interpretation is ideal for a child's winter coat. Experiment with other variations, using your imagination to form the reversed binding into suitable backgrounds for the buttons chosen.

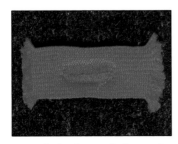

1 Mark the buttonhole on the reverse of the garment and overlay a piece of braid. Copy the mark and machine-sew a rectangle around it. Cut a slit and fray the ends of the braid.

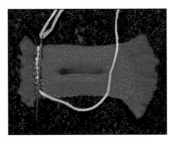

2 Ease the braid to the right side; press flat. Machine-sew along the edges of the braid and embroider stripes. On wrong side, oversew each end of buttonhole.

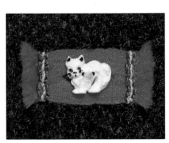

3 Sew the button onto a backing button on the wrong side of the button band to prevent pulling on the fabric.

Colorful Clay Buttons

Create your own unique and bright buttons out of colored thermosetting modeling clay, available from art and craft stores. The clay is first warmed and kneaded to make it pliable. To roll it out, use a smooth surface and a marble or china rolling pin, or even a bottle (the clay sticks to wood). Bake the results, following the manufacturer's instructions and supervising children at all times. Hand-wash the garments in lukewarm water, or remove the buttons before cleaning.

USEFUL EQUIPMENT

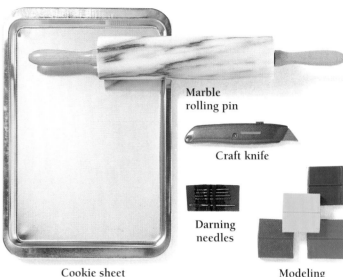

Marble rolling pin

Craft knife

Darning needles

Cookie sheet

Modeling clay supplied in blocks

MARBLED BUTTONS

Two or more colors are worked together to achieve random effects that perfectly complement abstract-patterned fabrics and yarns. Each finished button differs from every other, producing a special hand-crafted look.

1 Following the manufacturer's directions, warm two or more blocks of clay in different colors, and then knead them until soft.

2 Roll each piece into a long sausage shape, trying to ensure that both rolls are the same width, and twist the two together.

3 Knead the twist until a marbled effect is achieved. (If kneading is continued, the clays will blend to make a third color.)

4 Make a long roll, working the clay to an even thickness. When the roll reaches the desired diameter, slice disks from it using a sharp craft knife.

5 Reshape the disks, make the holes with a darning needle, and bake the buttons in an oven according to the manufacturer's instructions.

MILLEFIORI BUTTONS

This method is based on Venetian glass-making techniques. The aim is to create a roll of clay with the same pattern running all the way through it, like a stick of candy. Success depends on the evenness with which the clay is rolled. It is best to start with simple designs and to practice with small amounts of clay.

1 To make a stained-glass design, choose five colors for the central "panels" and a dark base color. Warm the clay, knead it, and work it into rolls.

2 Roll out a thin oblong of the base color, keeping the thickness as even as possible. Trim to size, and wrap a layer around each of the colored rolls.

3 Lay the rolls together as shown and form into one long, even roll. Cut this new roll into three pieces of equal length (or slice disks from it as in step 5).

4 Lay the three pieces together as shown and form into another long roll, keeping it even. As you do so, a more complicated pattern will emerge.

5 Once the roll is the right diameter for the buttons, slice off disks with a sharp craft knife and shape them if necessary. Avoid leaving fingerprints.

6 Make the holes with a darning needle, trying to avoid overhandling the buttons. Bake them according to the manufacturer's instructions.

Decorative Fastenings

Superb against velvets, brocades, and satins, fastenings such as frogging, loops, and Turk's-head knots provide a luxurious finishing touch for special occasions and evening wear. Made from cord, they can be satin or matte, thick or thin. Upholsterers are an excellent source of decorative cords. These fastenings should be dry-cleaned only.

FROGGING

Originally called Brandenburgs after the German town in which they first appeared on military uniforms in the late 1600s, these fastenings have remained popular. They are often applied in rows down the front of smoking jackets, oriental-style dresses, and Cossack coats.

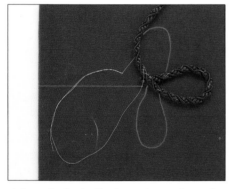

1 In tailor's chalk, draw the outline of the frog and cut a piece of cord long enough to make the whole shape. Start at the center and form the first loop. Tack it in place.

2 Following the marked design, make the second and third loops, ensuring that they are the same size, and tack them in place.

3 Tacking as you go, pass the cord under the third loop; continue to the edge of the garment. Make a smaller loop (to fasten over a button) and return the cord to the center. Cut the end and stitch it under the frog at the center.

4 Sew the cord to the fabric; remove the tacking. Sew on a covered button (see p. 70); exactly beneath it, under the facing, attach a button of the same size.

5 Repeat steps **1** to **4** on the other side. (When the frog is fastened, the second loop fastens underneath, onto the button at the back.)

TURK'S-HEAD KNOTS

Reminiscent of turbans, these cord buttons are derived from Eastern costume. Simple to make, they are the perfect complement to loops (see below) and give any garment a sumptuous feel. Practice making them with single cord first before trying with double. The size of the knot depends on the thickness of the cord used.

1 Cut a piece of cord long enough to make the whole knot. Leaving a length of cord on the right-hand side, make the first loop.

2 Make the second loop by going over the first one, then under the loose end.

3 Continue around, going over the second loop and under the first. While weaving, shape the cord into a ball, working the cord around to make a tight knot.

4 Overlap the lengths of cord at the base of the knot and secure with fabric glue. Cut the cord short and stitch into the knot to make a flat base.

LOOPS

A row of loops is elegant on a sleeve or bodice. Turk's-head knots or ball buttons work best with loops, but must be of the correct size to prevent the fastening from coming undone. This is especially true for shiny ball buttons and knots made with satin cord, which can easily slip.

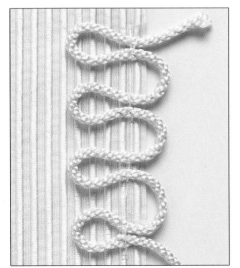

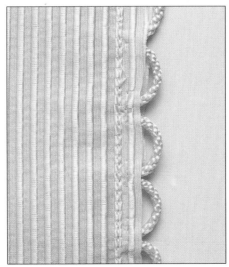

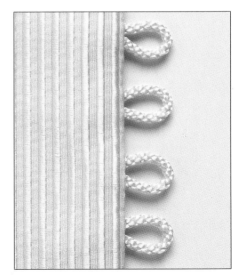

1 Make loop shapes (each the same size) on the right side of the fabric with one piece of cord; space at regular intervals. Tack at the base of each loop.

2 Sew on the facing, ensuring that the machine stitches firmly through the cord at the base of each loop. To be sure, sew down the facing twice.

3 Fold the facing over to the wrong side of the garment and press. To finish, attach buttons or Turk's-head knots to the opposite side of the garment.

Covered Buttons

Fabric-covered buttons can be used decoratively on pockets and cuffs as well as for fastening. Finished in the same cloth as the garment, they are subtly elegant; in a contrasting fabric, they can match other details, such as piping. Embroidery or lined lace are luxurious options for a special look.

COVERING KIT BUTTONS

Button molds in many sizes are available as kits. Metal bases (shown here) are suitable for large sizes and heavy fabrics; plastic is better for small buttons and delicate fabrics.

1 Cut the fabric as shown, using one layer for heavy fabrics, two layers or one layer plus lining for fine. Put the top part of the button mold in the center.

2 Fold the fabric around the mold, pressing the fabric onto the teeth so that they grip it firmly.

3 Push in the button base (making sure all the edges of the fabric are well tucked in) to hold the fabric securely in place.

BALL BUTTONS

Although this shape is not available in kit form, plastic ball buttons are easy to cover, making them ideal for dressy clothes.

1 Cut the fabric to size as for step 1 above and do a running stitch around the edge. Position the button in the center.

2 Pull the thread evenly so that the fabric wraps around the button and the edges are pulled tight next to the shank.

3 Finish off by oversewing through the edges of the fabric and into the shank to hold the fabric in place.

Index

Suppliers & Museums

UNITED STATES

STORES

Buttons by David
RD3, Box 375
Georgetown, Del. 19947
(302) 856–7569
Buttons for home sewing.

Regent Fabrics
122 East 59th Street
New York, N.Y. 10022
(212) 355–2039
*Three million buttons in stock
— old, new, and unusual.*

Renaissance Buttons
826 West Armitage
Chicago, Ill. 60614
(312) 883–9508
*Antique, vintage, collectible,
and modern buttons. Mail order
on purchases over $25.*

Tender Buttons
143 East 62nd Street
New York, N.Y.
(212) 758–7004
*A full range of buttons —
antique, new, and novelty.*

ASSOCIATIONS

National Button Society
Lois Pool, Secretary
2733 Juno Place
Akron, Ohio 44333
(216) 864–3296
*Membership $15 annually.
Receive the* National Button
Society Magazine *five times a
year. Meet with other collectors
at exhibitions and meetings.*

MUSEUMS

**Cooper-Hewitt National
Museum of Design**
2 East 91st Street
New York, N.Y. 10128
(212) 860–6898
*Extensive collection of buttons,
from the Renaissance to
modern times.*

Strong Museum
1 Manhattan Square
Rochester, N.Y. 14607
(716) 263–2700
*Very large, diverse button
collection.*

CANADA

WESTERN

Dressew Supply Ltd.
Vancouver, BC
(604) 682–6196
*Buttons, trims, fittings, and craft
supplies.*

Salmagundi West
Vancouver, BC
(604) 681–4648
*Beads, novelties, and craft
supplies.*

Artifax
Calgary, AB
(403) 244–9395
From 1920s to 1950s.

**Magowan's Oldwares &
Antiques**
Saskatoon, SK
(306) 653–4033
Pre-1950s.

The Curiosity Shop
Winnipeg, MB
(204) 943–2734
From 1900 on.

CENTRAL & ATLANTIC

Logan Antiques
Ottawa, ON
(613) 233–8943
Art Nouveau and Deco.

Dressmaker's Supply
Toronto, ON
(416) 922–6000
Over 15,000 designs.

Maryan's Fabrics Ltd
Toronto, ON
(416) 488–6111
Swiss and handmade Italian.

Blue Pillow Antiques
Montréal, PQ
(514) 871–0225
*Sterling Art Nouveau, brass,
porcelain, late Victorian.*

Drags
Montréal, PQ
(514) 866–0631
From 1940s to1960s.

Canterbury Antiques
St. John, NB
(506) 633–7038

Acknowledgments

Author's acknowledgments
I am extremely grateful to all my suppliers, family, and friends, and would like to thank them all for their practical assistance, advice, and moral support during the compilation of this book. First of all, much love and thanks go to my husband Michael for his patience and encouragement. Special thanks to my staff at Button Box — Sue Winter, Bill Harris, Jasette Amos, and Valerie Olleon — for their marvelous supportive assistance.

Many thanks to Toni Frith at The Button Queen, London; Eileen Helmer of The Magpie, Totnes; Jessie Partt of Western Antique Market, Bath; and Sheila Bird in Dorset — all of whom lent me beautiful antique buttons from their personal collections and shared their knowledge of the subject with me. (*Antique Buttons* pp. 28–9.)

Thanks also to Julia Hill and Sandra Duvall of Miro Buttons for their handmade buttons shown on pp. 30–1, and to Claire Grove in Cardiff for supplying examples and imparting her knowledge of making handmade buttons on pp. 66–7. Thanks to Mr. Riddle of the London Badge and Button Company Ltd. for the loan of metal buttons and for sharing his valuable knowledge with me; and to Val and Ray Atkinson at Azea Buttons for loaning

me the beautiful buttons handmade by aborigines.
For all their kindness and helpful assistance, thanks to Elizabeth Hess, Judy Stevenson, and Gavin Morgan at the Museum of London; Mr. Harvey at the Victoria and Albert Museum; Anna Meredith at the City of Birmingham Museum and Art Gallery; and the staff at the Dorset County Museum.

Thanks and love to Mollie and Ernest Whittemore for their indefatigable research; again to Mollie Whittemore, who designed and executed the beautiful examples of decorated and bound buttonholes on pp. 64–5, and loving thanks to my sister Claire for all her help.

Thanks to Terry Meinrath for invaluable information and the loan of samples, and to Tony Allen and Valerie Olleon for making up examples on pp. 64–5 and 68–9.

Grateful thanks to Mrs. Nichols, who kindly loaned me Mr. Nichols's original and unique couturier buttons from the 1940s, 1950s, and 1960s (triangle buttons on p. 49).

For providing all the yarns on pp. 48–9, warm thanks to Joanna Bawden of Colourspun, Camden Town; also for the loan of her mother's original Arts and Crafts buttons.

Love and thanks to Dave Acherman, Steve Pringle, and Malcolm Brown, who have, in their own special ways, made unique contributions to my life and career.

Particular thanks to Daphne Razazan for her understanding, enthusiasm, and direction, and for giving me this creative project at this time; and to Laura Harper, Tracey Clarke, and Carole Ash for their tireless patience, unfailing good humor, and for being such a great team to work with.

Lastly, a special thank you to Paul Hughes for locking me up to finish the book.

Dorling Kindersley would like to thank Susannah Marriott, Corinne Hall, and Mark Ronan for their editorial help; Steve Painter and Kate Sarluis for design assistance; Tim Ridley for photographs on pp. 54–5, 58–9, and 60–1; Sarah Ashun for photographic assistance; Hilary Bird for the index; Clive Webster for picture research; and Valerie Hooper for the garments on pp. 58–9. Thanks also to Liberty's and Johnny Paige at Fine Dress Fabrics for supplying the fabric samples on pp. 36–47.